Resource Management

Wiley Series on Systems Engineering and Analysis
Harold Chestnut

Resource Management

AN ALTERNATIVE VIEW OF THE MANAGEMENT PROCESS

Paul S. Bender

A Wiley-Interscience Publication

JOHN WILEY & SONS

New York • Chichester • Brisbane • Toronto • Singapore

78056

Library of Congress Cataloging in Publication Data:

Bender, Paul S., 1936-
  Resources management.

  (Wiley series on systems engineering and analysis,
ISSN 0084-019X)
  "A Wiley-Interscience publication."
  Bibliography: p.
  Includes index.
  1. Industrial management.   I. Title.   II. Series.

HD31.B379 1982   658   82-13471
ISBN 0-471-08179-5

Printed in the United States of America

10 9 8 7 6 5 4 3 2 1

Dedicated to Niccolo Machiavelli,
the earliest philosopher of management,
who five hundred years ago realized that

> *There is nothing more difficult to attempt,*
> *more perilous to conduct,*
> *or more uncertain in its success,*
> *than to take the lead in the introduction*
> *of a new order of things.*
> *Because the innovator has for enemies*
> *all those who have done well*
> *under old conditions,*
> *and only lukewarm defenders*
> *in those who might do well*
> *under the new.*

SYSTEMS ENGINEERING AND ANALYSIS SERIES

In a society which is producing more people, more materials, more things, and more information than ever before, systems engineering is indispensable in meeting the challenge of complexity. This series of books is an attempt to bring together in a complementary as well as unified fashion the many specialties of the subject, such as modeling and simulation, computing, control, probability and statistics, optimization, reliability, and economics, and to emphasize the interrelationship among them.

The aim is to make the series as comprehensive as possible without dwelling on the myriad details of each specialty and at the same time to provide a broad basic framework on which to build these details. The design of these books will be fundamental in nature to meet the needs of students and practitioners and to ensure they remain of lasting interest and importance.

Foreword

Hardly anyone would disagree that business has entered a period characterized by radical changes and great uncertainties. Inflation, scarce resources, rapidly fluctuating markets, and worldwide competition are just a few of the symptoms, or causes, of the unstable business environment. At the same time, there is an air of bewilderment in many companies, large and small, about new informational and communications technologies—what they are, how they can be used to reduce planning uncertainties (and increase profits), and where they are headed.

In this book, Paul Bender has developed a new management philosophy that brings order to the confusion currently faced by many managers. The philosophy is a distillation and integration of an impressively wide variety of management and scientific facts and concepts, and of Mr. Bender's own experiences as a consultant and company executive. The viewpoint presented is consistent and compelling. It challenges the reader to ask the question, Would my current planning problems be resolved if I were to structure my thinking and organize my data-gathering and decision-making activities using resource management concepts? The answer should be affirmative in a surprising number of instances.

The reader will also profit from Mr. Bender's treatment of informational systems. Every company of any size now has these systems, but too many make inadequate use of them, particularly to assist decision making. The book provides concepts about data, information, and knowledge that help us to think correctly about them. It presents guidelines for designing management information systems and suggests organizational strategies for best utilizing them.

The role of quantitative methods and models in resource management is particularly emphasized in the book, and correctly so. It seems obvious that the most important use for informational systems is to assist managers in making decisions. Too often, though, data are collected only for accounting purposes. Important as they are, accounting analyses describe past history and are not related or sufficiently relevant to choosing future courses of action.

Quantitative models, realized as powerful "number crunchers" on computers, are the mechanisms for analyzing quantities of data to evaluate decision alternatives. Great progress in model generation, optimization, and application has been made in recent years. Their influence will undoubtedly continue to grow in the 1980s. Mr. Bender has done an excellent job in providing the reader with an intuitive feeling about the nature of quantitative models and their relevance to resource management problems.

JEREMY F. SHAPIRO

Professor of Operations Research
* and Management*
Sloan School of Management
Massachusetts Institute of Technology
Cambridge, Massachusetts
October 1982

Preface

The economic and political developments of the past decade have brought about a substantial change in the perspective of business management. The emergence of scarcities in traditional raw materials and energy sources has been dramatized by the formation of suppliers' cartels and accompanied by substantial price increases and uncertainties of supply.

At a macroeconomic level, those developments are reflected in the current revisions of Keynes' economic theories to attempt to explain the phenomenon known as stagflation, which is characterized by high inflation rates, high unemployment rates, low rates of economic growth, and low productivity. Those efforts are characterized by a school of economic thinkers known as "supply-side" economists. Unlike Keynesian economists, who attempt to affect demand and consumption, the new school concentrates on promoting supply and production, through tax cuts and other incentives that induce savings and business investment, to cope with stagflation.

That macroeconomic-level change is translated at the microeconomic level as a change away from the traditional "marketing principle," prompting business people to change their outlook from an almost exclusive concern with demand satisfaction to a more rigorous allocation and administration of resources available in order to satisfy the demands of those market segments that can yield maximum benefits in the long term. The increased concern with resource availability and utilization is bringing about a reaction characterized by important changes in the manner in which companies are organized, and in their approaches to strategic and tactical planning and control.

The years ahead will witness exponential changes in all areas of human endeavor. As a consequence, experience will become increasingly irrelevant in dealing with the future. We will see with increasing frequency how the successful approaches of the past become the sources of the problems of the future. Thus, we are confronted with a future characterized by increasing uncertainty and complexity.

The search for business profitability under conditions of increasing uncertainty and complexity has brought about the need to rethink many of the classical approaches to business structure and operation and to change business perspective. Among the major changes in business perspective there are three that hold especial importance because of their potential long-range implications:

1. The replacement of the marketing principle by the resource management principle, to account for the increasing importance of supply constraints. This development, together with the expansion of the physical distribution concept into business logistics, and of the latter into physical resource management, bringing together all logistic and production functions, will result in a reduction of the *relative* importance of the marketing function, and a concomitant increase in the relative importance of logistic–production operations.

2. The intense use of informational resources to trade off against other resources in order to reduce the impact of the increasing costs of other resources will result in drastically different forms of business structure and operation.

3. The need to plan and manage business operations on a worldwide basis to gain economies of scale and scope will be an indispensable requisite for enterprises to remain competitive even in their traditional markets.

Our viewpoint here is that the combined effect of those changes makes it desirable to adopt a new approach to the analysis of business structure and operation. The approach proposed here focuses on the *resources* that an enterprise must manage to accomplish its mission, rather than on the classical *functions* that have been until now characteristic of business activity. Thus, business functions will be structured around the requirements for resource management. An important advantage of this approach is that a business can be described in terms that are easy to relate to larger aggregates: industries, the national economy, or the world economy.

The purpose of this book is to present an approach to business management based on the optimal trade-off between requirements that should be satisfied and the resources available to satisfy them. This approach then does not concentrate on any particular aspect of business operations but instead considers the entire system, characterized by the demands on it, the constraints and conditions that it must respect, and the costs and revenues associated with its operating processes.

Our aim is to describe the basic concepts behind this approach, as well as the techniques available to implement it in practical situations. The emphasis in the presentation varies in inverse proportion with the literature available on different subjects. Thus, we discuss at greater length those aspects and techniques not covered in enough detail in other sources, and we outline and provide bibliographical guidance on those topics that have been discussed at length in other publications.

This book is addressed to practitioners concerned with corporate strategy, marketing, finance, production, information systems, and logistics. Other readers who are concerned with general management, administration, research and development, and human resources management may find the ideas proposed here useful in developing their future strategies.

By providing specific, practical information on the techniques available to analyze and solve the problems related to resource management, I expect the reader to learn when to use them effectively in real-life situations. I also expect that the guidance provided to the literature available on different aspects of the subject will facilitate further study and research on those topics.

I hope this book will provide a fresh new approach to some of the classical problems of management, thus stimulating the search for innovative ways to face today's situation and to deal with the challenges and opportunities of the future.

PAUL S. BENDER

New York
October 1982

Contents

List of Figures

List of Tables

Resource Management

1

Introduction

The three decades that followed the end of World War II constituted one of the most unusual periods in history, characterized by a unique set of circumstances:

The reconstruction of Europe and Japan presented substantial opportunities for investments that could bring high returns, in a short time, at low risks, to supply an enormous demand for most types of goods and services.

The availability of a single, stable currency capable of supporting world trade and of serving as standard for a system of fixed rates of exchange.

The presence of a country capable of maintaining order in international affairs.

The abundant supply of raw materials and energy at low prices.

The presence of a small world population totaling less than 2 billion in 1945, with a rather low level of expectations.

The availability of the necessary technology to take advantage of the conditions in existence at the time.

By the late 1970s, and certainly by 1980, the world situation had changed completely in every aspect mentioned above:

World markets for most goods and services were close to saturation, limiting the opportunities for significant profits and encouraging protectionistic measures, accompanied by multinational competition.

There was no single, stable currency capable of supporting world trade, and rates of exchange were floating.

No country or international organization had the capability to maintain order in international affairs.

Most raw materials and fuels were in scarce supply, selling at high prices, with precarious availability.

World population was in excess of 4 billion, growing toward 6 billion by

2000 and expected to stabilize at 10–15 billion in the first half of the twenty-first century.

The technology available was substantially different from that of 1945. Of especial importance was the availability of powerful technology for automated information processing, which was not in existence in 1945.

These massive changes in the political and economic situation of the world in the brief span of 35 years resulted in parallel changes in the business situation. To understand the new business situation, its future implications, and the technology available to manage it, it is useful to review the different components that determine the economic aspects of the business environment. Other aspects, such as the political, social, and cultural factors that influence business conditions, will be accounted for in our presentation through their economic impact.

1. THE ECONOMIC ENVIRONMENT

It is useful to classify all economic activity in four sectors:

1. *Primary sector*, comprising all agricultural activities, such as farming and cattle raising, plus extractive activities, such as forestry, fishing, and oil exploration. Organizations in the primary sector are predominantly engaged in the production of goods.

2. *Secondary sector*, comprising all manufacturing activities, such as the production of automobiles, processed foods, appliances, and cosmetics, plus all activities related to arts and crafts, such as handmade ceramics and leather goods. Organizations in the secondary sector are predominantly engaged in the transformation of goods.

3. *Tertiary sector*, comprising service activities, such as wholesaling, retailing, warehousing, transportation, banking, and insurance. Organizations in the tertiary sector are predominantly engaged in the distribution of goods and services.

4. *Quaternary sector*, comprising all activities related to the creation, use, and diffusion of knowledge and information. These include, for example, education, research and development, publishing, broadcasting, communications, telephone and postal services, data processing services, and management consulting. We will refer to such activities as the information business, or the knowledge business. The importance of the information business derives from the circumstance that in a post-industrial society information becomes the key resource

available to people. As we will see later, at greater length, information
is the resource that binds all resources.

Figure 1 contains approximate figures showing the trends for the last 100
years in the composition of the work force in the United States. It shows that
during that period the fraction of working population engaged in primary
sector activities decreased steadily from .43 to .02. Employment in the secondary sector was about constant, representing approximately .30 of the
working force until the 1920s, when it rose to represent .40 of the working
force around 1940, and since then has been declining steadily. Within the
tertiary sector, service activities comprised a steady .20 of the working population until the 1960s, and since then they increased to .27 by 1980. The
figures for the information business tell a dramatic story: from .09 of the
working population in 1880, employment grew to .50 by 1980 and is expected
to continue growing.

These trends illustrate what is one of the most important factors in the
world situation today: the emergence of an informational revolution propelled by simultaneous advances in computer, telecommunication, and television technologies. As happened before with the Agricultural Revolution
and with the Industrial Revolution, the Informational Revolution is bringing

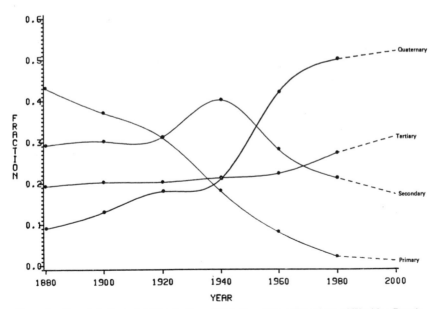

Figure 1. Trends in Sectorial Distribution of U.S. Population (Fractions of Working Population). Source: Adapted from U.S Department of Labor.

about critical problems, never experienced before, that affect the social, political, and economic aspects of our civilization. As also happened before, the new technologies that brought about the Informational Revolution will be the key to the solution of the problems derived from it. In later chapters of this book, we will discuss specifically how the new informational technologies can be applied to the new business conditions that have emerged as a consequence of the important social, political, and economic changes that are taking place in the world today as a consequence of the Informational Revolution.

The classification of industries into the four sectors discussed is useful because economic activities in each one of the sectors have substantial similarities and can thus be analyzed as groups from the standpoints of their resource requirements and their management requirements. Furthermore, the classification describes well the major stages of economic development of an economic system. Thus, preindustrial societies are characterized by economic activities that are predominantly in the primary sector: agriculture, fishing, and mining. As capital formation and technological sophistication increase, the economic system becomes industrialized, and economic activity shifts predominantly to the secondary sector—transformation of goods supplied by the primary sector. Subsequent advances in technology together with increased capital resources transform an industrial society into a postindustrial society, in which most of the economic activity takes place in the tertiary and quaternary sectors.

These conditions are clearly in evidence throughout the world today: the less developed countries have economies concentrated in the primary sector, the industrialized countries have economies concentrated in the secondary sector, and recently the U.S. economy has made the transition to a postindustrial system with major concentration in the tertiary and quaternary sectors.

As the world economy continues in a transition process and more countries shift to an industrial or postindustrial economy, we will be confronted with significant changes in the intensity and dispersion of demands for goods and services, as well as in the availability, reliability, and cost of supplies. These changes will have a major impact on the problems faced by business managers in the future.

Regardless of the stage of economic development in a particular society, all sectors of the economy must perform the same basic activities.

1.1. Activities

In their simplest form, economic activities can be described as an interaction between two sectors—a business sector and a market sector—to exchange products that can be physical goods or services. The business sector procures goods and services from supply markets, transforms them, and distributes the resulting goods and services to demand markets.

To facilitate our discussion, it is convenient to separate the supply side of the market sector from its demand side. Thus, we can extend our description of economic activities and depict it as a flow of goods and services that originated at supply markets, were procured by businesses that engage in the production of goods and services, and that are in turn distributed to demand markets. This process is described graphically in Figure 2, where we can identify the following economic activities:

1. *Supply*, which is the offer of goods and services for exchange.
2. *Procurement*, which is the activities related to identifying and selecting the sources of supply of needed products and to making the products available at the places where they are needed.
3. *Production*, which is the transformation of goods procured into different goods through physical, chemical, or biological processes, or their incorporation in service-rendering processes.
4. *Distribution*, which circulates the products resulting from production to make them available for exchange at demand markets.
5. *Demand*, which is the acquisition of products, either for final consumption or for investment, to generate new supplies.
6. *Investment*, which is the use of surplus demand not used for consumption to generate new supply.

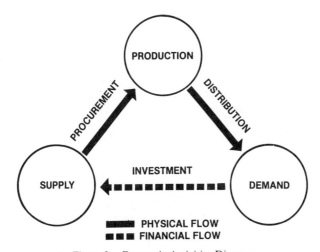

Figure 2. Economic Activities Diagram

1.2.   Resources

Economic activities can be described as the interaction, use, or exchange of four types of resources, each one comprising one or more kinds of resources, as follows:

1. *Human resources*, including all the people involved in economic activities.
2. *Physical resources*, including
   a. Land
   b. Facilities
   c. Equipment
   d. Materials and/or Energy.
3. *Financial resources*, including all other assets and liabilities, such as cash and accounts payable.
4. *Informational resources*, including
   a. Data
   b. Knowledge
   c. Software
   d. Hardware.

One of the most significant differences among the four different sectors of an economic system is that of their intensity of use of different resources. We can display these differences, identifying for each resource which sector has the highest (Hi), intermediate (Med), and lowest (Lo) requirement for it. Thus, we obtain Table 1.

1.3.   Protagonists

People are the main resource in an economic system. Therefore, to describe the business environment we must focus on the protagonists that give it its identity.

There are seven groups of people that interact in the business process. They are:

1. *Customers*, engaged in the demand activity of the economic system. Their requirements, and their geographic locations, constitute one of the basic factors in business management. Traditionally, U.S. business has been demand oriented; that is, the requirements of customers and prospects have been the point of departure of business plans. This is no longer so: current and projected business conditions indicate that demand requirements—although still a critical factor—are no

Table 1. *Comparative Intensity of Resource Use*

Resources		Sectors			
		Primary	Secondary	Tertiary	Quaternary
Human	(Education Level)	Lo	Med	Med	Hi
Physical	Land	Hi	Med	Lo	Lo
	Facilities	Med	Hi	Med	Lo
	Equipment	Med	Hi	Med	Lo
	Materials and/or Energy	Med	Hi	Lo	Lo
Financial	(Capital)	Med	Hi	Med	Lo
Informational	Data	Lo	Med	Hi	Hi
	Knowledge	Lo	Med	Med	Hi
	Software	Lo	Med	Med	Hi
	Hardware	Lo	Med	Med	Hi

7

longer the major factor to consider in planning and operating a business. The other protagonists involved have become equally important.

2. *Suppliers*, engaged in the supply activity of the economic system. Shortages and increasing prices of physical resources have increased significantly the importance of the supply side of the economy in business planning and operations.

3. *Employees*, engaged in the production activity of the economic system. By extension, they perform the allied functions of procurement, distribution, and investment. The availability of properly trained employees to perform those functions and activities is becoming an increasingly important constraint on business operations.

4. *Competitors* are simply employees working in a different business or sector of the economy. In developing a business strategy, the assessment of competitors' pressures and reactions is of critical importance. Because of the increasing complexity of the business environment, competitive analysis has become as important an element in business planning and operating as the evaluation of customers' requirements and suppliers' capabilities.

5. *Owners* of business financial resources. Their investment makes possible the operation of the business; in exchange, they require from the business an adequate return on their investment.

6. *Public* includes all the people living in the society in which a business operates and their political representatives.

These seven groups constitute the protagonists involved in all business activities. Any individual may belong to several or all of these categories, acting in different roles with regard to a given business.

1.4. Major Economic Variables and Trends

Numerous polls of senior international executives indicate a remarkable degree of agreement regarding what they consider to be the major economic variables, their trends, and their consequent effects on the business situation in the 1980s. A typical survey conducted in 1980 showed that the 12 most pressing problems expected to confront management in the industrialized countries during the 1980s were, in order of importance:

1. High rate of inflation
2. Low availability and high cost of labor
3. Low availability and high cost of energy

   4. Increasing government regulation
   5. Increasingly difficult management–labor relations
   6. Low availability of qualified managers
   7. Increasing pace of introduction of new technology
   8. Fluctuating exchange rates
   9. Low availability and high cost of raw materials
   10. Low availability and high cost of investment capital
   11. New competitors
   12. Increasing pressures from environmental groups

These problems constitute a fairly comprehensive description of the general conditions that are expected to prevail in the business environment of the 1980s. Although their causes are many and interrelate in complex ways, we can reduce them to exponential changes of four types: demographic, sociopolitical, economic, and technological.

The main characteristic of exponential change is that as changes occur, they occur with increasing speed. As a consequence, changes of equivalent magnitude occur faster than before. The major changes that business will be confronting in the 1980s are described in the following subsections.

Demographic Changes.   These are the root cause of all other changes occurring in the world. Since population growth rates and patterns have considerable inertia, it is possible to arrive at acceptably accurate forecasts of population levels for a reasonably short time period, such as the next 20 years. Independent population forecasts published by numerous organizations, such as the U.S. government and the United Nations, show remarkable agreement, pointing out that the world's population will grow from approximately 4 billion in 1975 to approximately 6.3 billion in 2000.

An increase in world population by a factor of about 1.6 within 25 years can be expected to produce a number of major alterations in the economic, social, and political conditions within which business will have to operate in the coming years. First, additional population will generate additional needs for food, energy, clothing, shelter, education, communications, and financial resources. Unless the world economy can meet those needs when they occur, serious problems will arise, creating increasing inflation, social turmoil, and political instability. The situation will be further complicated by the fact that projected population growth rates show significant disparities: the industrialized countries are expected to have minor population increases, whereas the less developed countries are expected to account for most of the population growth.

Significant changes in the number and distribution of world population will have major consequences for business. These will include:

1. *A realignment of demand markets throughout the world.* This can be expected to be accompanied by an increase in the demand for products and sevices related to the production and distribution of food, clothing, shelter, education, health, and other essentials. Given the financial constraints known at this time, likely consequences of this demand increase will be continued inflation and increasing social turmoil.

2. *A shift in the location of labor pools*, with most of the skilled workers concentrated in the industrialized countries and the bulk of the unskilled workers dispersed throughout the rest of the world. As a consequence, we can expect a growing trend toward a worldwide division of labor, in order to take advantage of local labor availability and costs. This work mode will require new, large logistic systems to ensure the efficient flow of materials between suppliers, producers, and consumers, as well as enhanced communications networks to support the additional informational flows needed to manage such operations.

Sociopolitical Changes. Exponential change translates into a number of sociopolitical changes of direct consequence to business. The most important of these are described in the following subsections.

Multipolar Political Arrangements. Until the mid-1970s worldwide political lines were drawn between two major camps, one dominated by the United States, the other by the Soviet Union. In the late 1970s additional political poles emerged, mainly in Western Europe, Japan, and China, that started to diffuse the world's political alignments. Since these constitute one of the underpinnings of world trade, we are currently witnessing the appearance of new trade patterns that will substantially alter the business environment in the 1980s and beyond. Among the most important of these are commercial relations between the United States and China and increased trade between Eastern and Western Europe and between Japan and all of the above. As additional political poles emerge in the future, potentially in such places as Brazil, and India, the complexity of trading patterns will increase further.

Political Instability. The late 1970s witnessed another major sociopolitical transformation in the world, in the emergence of politically unstable regimes in areas that had hitherto been stable, and almost dormant. Good examples can be found in several countries in Central and South America, in the Middle East, in the Far East, and in Eastern Europe.

The business consequences of such political instability have been major market realignments. A good illustration of this point is Iran, where U.S. companies had carved out major market shares in most industrial sectors until a change in Iran's regime brought about an almost overnight cessation of all commerce between the two countries. Suppliers from other countries went in to fill the void.

A cursory review of the political situation in many other areas of the world reveals a significant number of potential problem areas.

Single-Issue Lobbies. The increasing importance in the American political scene of single-issue lobbies as a major force behind new legislation is creating new political conditions that directly affect the business environment. The reason for the new political conditions is that lobbies, in contradistinction with political parties, seldom feel compelled to provide an all-encompassing view of the social, political, and economic implications of their limited aims. Thus, the consequences of their favored legislation in other areas of the economy or in sociopolitical alignments are usually ignored.

The actions of political lobbies create the real possibility of having to operate in a legal environment containing contradictory legislation. This adds to the complexity of the business environment.

Government Regulation. Another major sociopolitical change affecting the business environment is the increasing reach of government regulations in the conduct of business. In many industries, including automotive, drug, and food, critical decisions affecting product design and marketing strategy are almost predetermined by existing regulations. Since changes in regulations are seldom predictable, this adds an element of increasing uncertainty in the business environment.

Role of Women. The role of women is increasing substantially, as illustrated by the fact that the fraction of women of working age in the workforce has increased from about .20 in 1950 to about .43 in 1980. This not only requires an acceleration of economic growth to create much more employment, but also is changing relations in the work place.

Impact of Massive Information. With the general availability of television and the increasing access to large data bases through home computers, people are able to acquire a much higher level of knowledge and vicarious experience than was the case only a few years ago. As a consequence, people in the work force have higher expectations and feel more qualified to participate in the decisions that affect their work. This situation requires new ways to structure, motivate, and direct people working in organizations.

Economic Changes. The third area experiencing exponential changes is the economic area, where we are witnessing the trends described in the following subsections.

Services. As explained before, economic systems exhibit a secular trend toward services. This trend is manifested by an increasing fraction of the working population being transferred to service-related occupations, whereas a decreasing fraction of workers is engaged in agricultural, extractive, and manufacturing activities. The speed with which this trend is taking place is creating serious employment dislocations, since there is a significant time lag involved in retraining and generally reabsorbing displaced workers within the economic system. Another major consequence of this trend, together with the demographic changes outlined before, is a transition toward an international division of labor.

International Division of Labor. This trend is already evident in many industries, such as steel, automobiles, textiles, apparel, and shoes. These industries are migrating away from the industrialized nations of North America, Japan, and Europe and toward emerging industrial centers in Asia, Africa, and Latin America. In general, we can expect that labor-intensive industries will be relocating to areas with high population and relatively lower incomes and that capital- and knowledge-intensive industries will tend to develop predominantly in the already-industrialized areas.

This reallocation of industrial activity is not only efficient from an economic point of view but also desirable from a social standpoint: it will allow the creation of new employment in the areas where such need will be most acute. A major consequence of this change will be the emergence of much more complex, worldwide logistics and information systems to support this type of economic activity.

Scarcity of Traditional Resources. The growing scarcity of many traditional raw materials and fuels is producing two major economic reactions. First, it is fueling inflation, as increasing world demand is met with stable or shrinking supply. Second, it is producing a significant reallocation of resources to develop replacements and improve utilization of such raw materials and fuels, and thus introducing new technologies into the economic process.

Financial Reallocation. Since the end of 1973 we have witnessed a massive transfer of financial resources from the industrialized nations to the oil-producing nations. This process is likely to continue during the coming years. As a result major new financial centers are emerging in the world, and as some of that capital is invested locally, new industrial bases are being created from scratch in new areas of the world, especially the Middle East and some African and Latin American nations. These new production sources are already beginning to alter the world supply conditions in many industries, such as petrochemicals. This trend can be expected to intensify in the coming years, thus sensibly altering the characteristics of world markets.

Technological Changes. These include:

Intensified Use of Scientific Management Technology. One of the outcomes of the increasing importance of the knowledge-related industries has been the increasingly faster development and introduction of scientific management technology in the management process. This trend has been compounded by the availability of more powerful, cheaper computers that enable their practical application in business. This is reflected in the increasingly sophisticated and successful use of operations research techniques to guide managerial decision making at all levels of business, in the economically successful countries.

As a consequence of this trend, we are witnessing improving effectiveness in resource management throughout the economy. This has been accompanied by a clear trend toward more delegation in the decision-making process—decisions such as determining inventory investment levels that used to be the exclusive province of top mangement—have now been delegated to middle management. This has been accomplished through the use of highly sophisticated automated decision support systems.

Technological Breakthroughs. The 1980s are witnessing a major revolution in scientific thinking that is beginning to have major technological and, therefore economic, impact. Our entire conception of how the universe is structured, and how it works, is changing dramatically. The research being conducted in many different fields, such as Ilya Prigogine's work on physical chemistry, Eric Jantsch's work on evolution of systems, and Karl Pribram's work on thinking processes, are not only providing totally new views of the universe but also contributing to the generation of whole new technologies.

If history is any guide, these new views are likely to have a major impact in political and social developments in the years to come, increasing the complexity of the sociopolitical problems already discussed. Furthermore, we can expect whole new industries to emerge, applying the new technologies to create totally new products, or substantially alter the characteristics of existing ones. Some of the most important new industries that are emerging include:

Bioengineering-based industries to produce synthetic living organisms capable of performing industrial operations, in entirely new ways.

Microelectronics developments that will enable the construction of new, dramatically more powerful microprocessors of very small sizes. This will enable the development of products with a high level of built-in intelligence and will provide significant improvement in the benefit–cost ratio of computers. One area of major importance in this regard is robotics, or the technology to produce highly skilled robots capable of performing a wide variety of industrial operations with high speed and accuracy at low cost.

Photonics, or the utilization of light instead of electric currents as signaling medium. This technology will have a significant impact on how information is stored, processed, transmitted, and displayed.

1.5. Business Consequences

The exponential changes discussed above produce a number of consequences in the business environment. These consequences are reflected in three major trends, described in the following subsections.

Increasing Uncertainty.   This trend is a direct consequence of the exponential nature of changes taking place in the world. These changes are clearly illustrated by the behavior of numerous economic time series, such as those presented in Figures 3 and 4. An examination of those long-term time series indicates that the changes described in the following subsections are taking place:

Breaks in Long-Range Trends.   Trends that lasted for many years suddenly become invalid, as shown in Figure 3, displaying the behavior of U.S. savings rate, and Figure 4, displaying U.S. consumer installment debt outstanding.

Oscillations of Growing Amplitude.   Cyclical and seasonal phenomena are becoming unstable, as shown by the growing amplitude of the cycle shown in Figure 5, displaying the behavior of the consumer Price Index for all items in the United States.

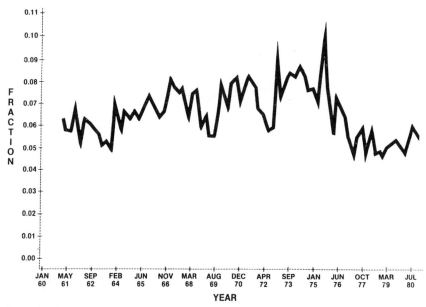

Figure 3. Personal Saving Rate (Fraction Per Year). Source: U.S. Department of Commerce.

Dissipating Correlations. Economic variables that formerly were highly correlated suddenly show decreasing or vanishing correlation. One of the most dramatic examples of dissipating correlations is that of the Phillips curve, which relates inversely the level of inflation to the level of unemployment in a given country. For many years that relationship appeared to be a law of economics, until in the late 1960s it simply ceased to work. At that time it became clear that prevailing economic conditions were such that increasing inflation was being accompanied by increasing rather than decreasing unemployment.

Increasing Complexity. From our previous discussion on expected management problems in the 1980s we can see that the majority of such problems derive from several basic causes, treated in the following subsections.

Growing Number of Interacting Variables. Many business parameters that were held constant—such as currency exchange rates—or used to change at a slow pace—such as inflation—are no longer constant or changing slowly. Similarly, the plentiful availability and low cost of key resources, such as energy, raw materials, and skilled labor, which were taken for granted until a few years ago, have become major constraining variables to be considered

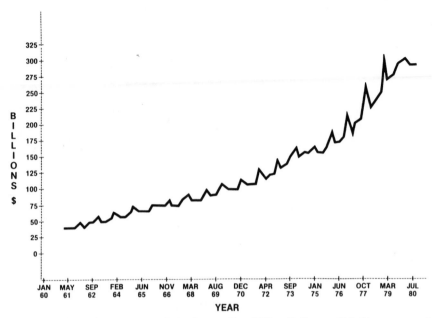

Figure 4. Consumer Installment Debt Outstanding (Billion $). Source: U.S. Department of Commerce.

explicitly. Similarly, growing pressures from minority, environmental, safety, and other lobbies, added to significant diversification of competition, result in problems that are much more complex than those of only a decade ago.

Internationalization of Economic Activity. The improvements in communications and transportation systems that have taken place in the last few decades have made it practical and profitable for a growing number of companies to view their operations in a multinational, global context. Thus, in most countries of the world we witness enlarged competition for domestic markets between the local companies that traditionally served them and foreign companies that penetrate those markets. Furthermore, since effective global operations demand an international division of labor and multinational investment policies, the nature of local production and financing arrangements is changing drastically in most countries.

Increasing Size and Scope of Companies and Governments. Another reason for the growing complexity of business problems is the increasing concentration of business into larger corporations that often control cash flows larger than those of many nations. Such organizations, frequently operating in many different lines of business, in many countries, are creating new legal, financial, and operational conditions. Managing such companies, or competing with them, is an increasingly complex problem for managers.

A parallel development has been the growing size and scope of national governments, which are becoming involved in more detailed aspects of the economy through a continuously increasing number of laws and regulations that constrain business operations and reduce the options open to management. Since the content, scope, and timing of new laws and regulations are difficult to forecast, this element also increases the level of uncertainty under which management must operate.

Persistent Inflation. The third major trend we are witnessing is that of a persistently high—by historical standards—rate of inflation. This trend is clearly shown in Figure 5, where we see that the 20-year trend in consumer prices has clearly been increasing at an exponential rate.

There are many possible scenarios that could suddenly produce a reversal of this trend from inflation to deflation. These include a major war or any other sudden occurrences that might precipitate a major economic depression. However, throughout history the long-term trend has been toward inflation; thus, we can expect this to be true in the future, even if the overall

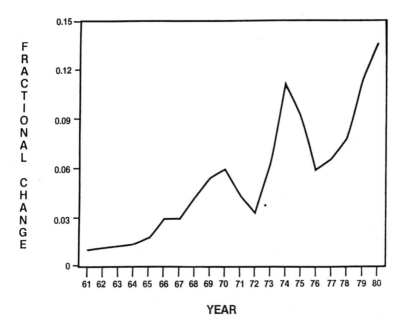

Figure 5. Consumer Price Index (All Items). Source: U.S. Department of Commerce

trend sometimes abates or is punctuated by sporadic reversals. The main reason supporting this viewpoint is that we will continue to witness decreasing supply of traditional resources, and at the same time there will be increasing demands for them because of increases in population.

On the other hand, if we look at the trend of unit costs of data processing hardware, as shown in Figure 12, we see that it has *decreased* from 126 cents per 100,000 multiplications in 1952, to less than .1 cent in 1980, or a compounded annual rate of decrease of about .3. With the advent of mass-produced microprocessors, we can expect this trend to continue for the foreseeable future, as these devices replace traditional computers.

Let us now examine how the application of informational resources to the management process will make it possible to manage under conditions of increasing uncertainty and complexity and persistent inflation.

Managing under Increasing Uncertainty.   In order to accomplish this, management systems must provide the elements detailed in the following subsections.

Adaptability.   This capability enables easy evolution in a continuously changing environment. It ensures that management systems can be continuously updated to deal with the real problems faced by an organization, instead of with yesterday's problems, which may have become irrelevant.

Skill Amplification.   This is the capability to provide people with management systems that can significantly extend and improve their accuracy, speed, and memory when dealing with problems. It enables management to reposition a system quickly, as well as to perform all necessary tasks, with high levels of data accuracy and completeness.

Contingency Planning.   This is the capability to develop and maintain up-to-date plans for dealing with alternative scenarios that encompass the range of possible situations the organization may face. It serves to identify actions that must be taken to keep the organization in a state of readiness and therefore increases its reaction speed.

Managing under Increasing Complexity.   In order to achieve this, management systems must have the abilities described in the following subsections.

Skill Transferring.   This capability enables a large number of relatively unskilled people to apply powerful problem-solving techniques, developed by a small number of highly skilled experts. It expands an organization's ability to respond effectively to highly complex issues at all levels.

Sensitivity Analysis. This ability enables the calculation of the range within which problem parameters can vary without changing the structure of the solution. This feature allows managers to quantify the relative importance of the parameters that describe a problem: the narrower the range within which a parameter can vary without affecting the solution, the more important it is to obtain accurate estimates of it.

Management by Exception. This approach enables managers to establish control limits for the value of each parameter in a problem and to concentrate management attention on those parameters that fall outside the control limits. It allows them to direct most of their efforts toward the few parameters that have a major influence on the outcome of a situation or the solution of a problem. Thus, complex problems involving the interactions of many parameters can be effectively managed by the selective application of management resources where they count most.

Managing under Persistent Inflation. In order to accomplish this, systems must be oriented toward the measures described in the following subsections.

System Trade-Offs. Management systems must focus on maximizing total system benefits, not the benefits associated with each separate part of the system.

Trade-offs can be of two types:

Cost–Cost trade-offs, which are obtained from exchanges between several cost and revenue elements in the system.

Performance–Cost trade-offs, which are obtained from exchanges between the performance or service provided by the system and the costs involved in providing it.

Since different cost and revenue elements vary at different rates, and since optimal performance provided by a system varies with fluctuating market conditions, it is important to provide managers with the tools needed to recalculate periodically the best trade-offs to maintain the organization's profitability at the highest level consistent with ongoing costs, constraints, and conditions. Furthermore, in order to obtain the greatest possible benefit, it is necessary to involve in the trade-off analysis as many elements as possible, to maximize the extent of possible trade-offs.

Economies of Scale and Scope. A second type of strategy to cope with inflation is the use of management systems that take advantage of opportunities for economies of scale and scope. Those systems can help management identify such opportunities and then establish the best organization structure and resource allocation to provide additional system trade-offs, as well as to decrease costs. How this can be accomplished is described in the following discussion.

Economies of scale can be obtained through:

Centralization of activities either on a functional or a geographic basis. This results in better utilization of personnel and equipment.

Consolidation of operations, to reduce overhead.

Learning effect, whereby as the number of items produced—or times an operation is performed—increases, the time needed for subsequent items, or operations, declines.

Specialization of activities, either vertically—through delegation—or horizontally—through division of labor. Specialization is basically a method to accentuate the impact of learning.

Economies of scope can be obtained by:

Integration of activities, which can be either *vertical*, by enlarging the stages of a process and thus producing additional trade-off opportunities, or *horizontal*, by enlarging the size of a process and thus producing additional economies of scale.

Conglomeration of operations, or lateral integration whereby several organizations are merged, thus creating opportunities to share common assets, such as a sales force, transportation equipment, manufacturing and logistic facilities, data communications and processing facilities. This produces cost reductions through improved utilization of such assets and diversifies risk.

Simplification of product design to offer fewer features or options, thus obtaining cost reductions without significant reductions in performance.

Standardization of products and components, which allows production of fewer varieties in consequently larger quantities and reduces the inventory investment needed for a given level of service.

Substitution of materials through a continuous program of value analysis, to ensure that products perform at a desired level while being manufactured with the cheapest components compatible with such level.

Productivity improvement, which can be achieved by any of the approaches outlined above, plus the following strategy.

Automation of work processes that enable the exchange of information-related costs for time-, human-, financial-, and physical-resources-related costs.

Work redesign, to ensure that all tasks are performed with maximum efficiency. To that end, it is necessary not only to employ the classical industrial engineering techniques for work design but also to give substantial attention to the application of behavioral sciences in order to design work that enhances worker satisfaction and motivation.

1.6. Dealing with Projected Business Trends and Conditions

The business consequences of exponential changes will induce significant changes in the approaches to management issues in the future. The new conditions we can expect in the years to come will certainly require new ideas in order for us to cope successfully with them.

Our viewpoint in this book is that the new approaches in business management will hinge on three major ideas.

1. Informational resources will become the central resources of management.
2. The marketing principle will be replaced by the resource management principle, which is discussed at length in later chapters.
3. Businesses will have to operate on a worldwide basis in order to survive and prosper.

Since the central theme behind these three ideas is that of resource management, we need to define the resources involved in the management process. Our approach will be to focus on four types of resources that must be managed within a fifth: time. The four resource types we are concerned with are:

Physical resources, including

Land used for cultivation, extraction, or to contain facilities.

Facilities, for production, logistics, or administration.

Equipment, for production, logistics, or administration. These are devices that can perform physical work, such as machine tools, rail cars, lift trucks, or filing cabinets.

Materials, including raw materials and in-process and finished goods, as well as energy, supplies, and, in some cases, water and air.

Financial resources, including all other assets, such as cash and accounts receivable, and all other liabilities, such as accounts payable.

Human resources, including all protagonists involved in an organization's activities.

Informational resources, including the organization's data, knowledge, software, and hardware. The last category includes all programmable devices whose primary characteristic is the emulation of thinking processes; these include microprocessors, computers, communications devices, text processors and industrial robots.

Let us now review the three major ideas stated above.

Informational Resources Will Become the Central Resources of Management. We have seen in Figure 1 that as an economic system matures there is an increasing transfer of workers from other sectors to the informational sector. There is also an increase in their per capita income. This suggests a principle that we can state as follows: the higher the knowledge content of an economic activity, the higher its productivity. Information systems are the means through which knowledge is applied to the economic process. This is the main reason why the massive use of informational resources in human activity will become the key to effective management in the years to come, as an increasing fraction of the work force migrates to information-related activities.

Another important reason why informational resources will become the central resources of management is cost trends. If we examine long-term trends in costs representative of each major resource, we find that between 1961 and 1980:

> Labor unit costs increased by a factor of 3.7, as shown in Figure 6, containing annual U.S. hourly compensation per hour worked in the private business sector.
>
> Financial unit costs increased by a factor of 2.7, as shown in Figure 7, containing average annual corporate bond yields as reported by Moody's.
>
> Land unit costs increased by a factor of 5.9, as shown in Figure 8, containing average farm land prices.
>
> Facilities unit costs increased by a factor of 3.4, as shown in Figure 9, containing the nonresidential structure price deflator.
>
> Equipment unit costs increased by a factor of 2.2, as shown in Figure 10, containing the equipment price deflator.
>
> Industrial raw material unit costs increased by a factor of 2.9, as shown in Figure 11, containing the Wholesale Price Index for industrial commodities.

Although the long-term prices of physical, financial, and human resources increased at the rates mentioned, the cost of information processing, as shown in Figure 12, decreased at a compounded annual rate of about .3. Thus, it is clear that in order to contain increases in total costs it is essential

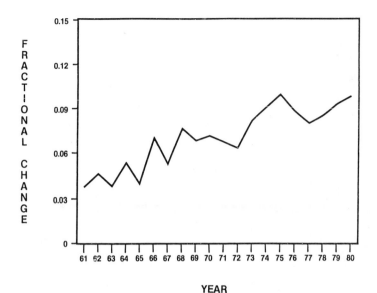

Figure 6. Compensation Per Hour Worked (Private Business Sector). Source: U.S. Department of Labor.

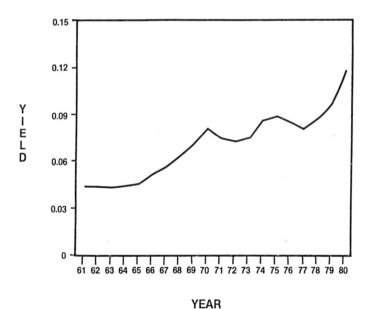

Figure 7. Moody's Corporate Bond Yields. Source: U.S. Department of Commerce.

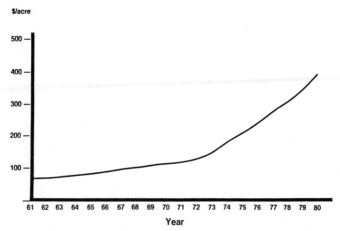

Figure 8. Land Price Trend (Average Farmland Value). Source: U.S. Department of Agriculture.

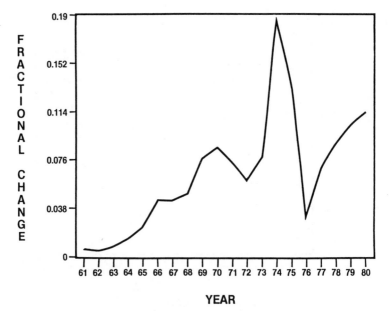

Figure 9. Nonresidential Structures Price Deflator. Source: U.S. Department of Commerce.

24

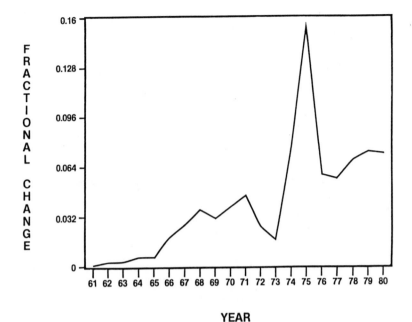

Figure 10. Equipment Price Deflator. Source: U.S. Department of Commerce.

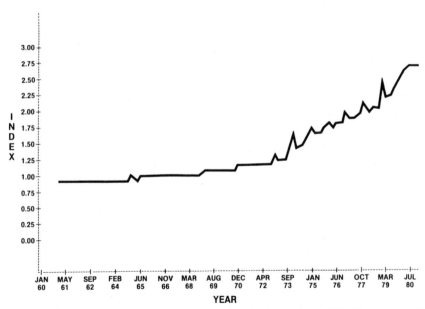

Figure 11. Wholesale Price Index (Industrial Commodities). Source: U.S. Department of Commerce.

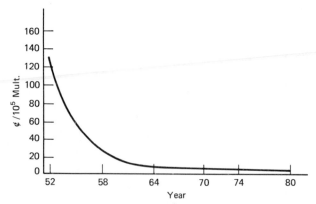

Figure 12.   Data Processing Hardware Unit Cost. Source: IBM Corporation.

continuously to implement ways to trade informational resources against all other resources. These trade-offs can take many forms, but essentially they fall into one of three major categories, described in the following subsections.

Management System Automation.   This category encompasses activities related to planning, executing, and controlling business processes. These include production planning and control, inventory management, accounting, portfolio management, resource allocation, and sales planning and control, for example. Typical consequences of management system automation are:

Improved facility and equipment utilization, through more efficient plans and better controls. This results in additional output from the same facility or piece of equipment.

Reduced inventories for a given level of service, through more effective inventory management systems. This results in lower investment in inventories and less space requirements for storage facilities.

Improved personnel utilization, through the automation or elimination of routine manual calculations and decisions and better personnel scheduling and control. This results in additional output per labor hour, with a consequent decrease in labor costs.

Process Automation.   This category encompasses activities related to the execution and coordination of plans and directives, in production and logistic operations. These include the use of miniprocessors and microprocessors, numerically controlled machines, robots, and computer-aided design and manufacturing techniques, for example. Typical consequences of process automation are:

Improved materials and energy utilization, through on-line monitoring of processes. This results in additional output for a given amount of materials and fuels and in significant reductions in the level of quality rejects. Both of these results produce lower material and energy costs.

Improved personnel utilization, through the automation of most operations and control functions in production and logistic processes. This results in additional output per labor hour, the elimination of many functions, and a reduction in operating errors, with consequent reductions in labor costs.

Data Management Automation. This category encompasses automated means for data storage, retrieval, communications, display, and text processing. Typical consequences of data management automation are:

Faster data transmission and availability, through electronic speed processing. This results in shorter response times, with a consequent improvement in customer service, and reduced financial floats.

Increased versatility in data input and output, through the use of video and audio techniques, such as electronic wand and voice input and graphic and voice output. This results in lower skill requirements to interact with information systems and more effective exchange of information between people and automated systems, with a consequent improvement in decision making and work quality at lower organizational levels.

The informational trade-off approaches outlined above result in the exchange of higher informational costs against substantially lower costs in physical, human, and financial resources. Furthermore, better service and improved decision-making quality enhance even more the desirability of such trade-offs. More specifically, the use of automated informational technology provides a most effective way of coping with increasing uncertainty and complexity and persistent inflation by satisfying the major requirements of management systems, which were discussed before. These are the reasons why informational resources are becoming the central resources of management.

The Marketing Principle Will Be Replaced by the Resource Management Principle. The marketing principle is the approach that consists in identifying market needs and then marshaling the necessary resources to meet them profitably. The resource management principle is the approach that consists in identifying market needs, quantifying resources available, and then establishing the optimal way to match them.

The basic difference between the two principles is that the marketing principle assumes that resources are available and have an acceptable cost, whereas the resource management principle does not. As a consequence, their application takes a different form. The marketing approach is a linear, sequential analysis that starts from market needs and progressively determines all requirements needed to fulfill them. The resource management approach is a network, parallel analysis, where all factors must be considered simultaneously to arrive at the most advantageous strategy. Thus, the marketing approach is easier to apply but can lead to impractical alternatives when the assumptions about resource availability and cost are not correct. Since this is becoming the most common situation, we can expect in the next few years to see the replacement of the marketing principle.

It is important to notice that the marketing principle flourished during the years when Keynesian economics was the prevailing orthodoxy. Their decline in popularity has also come at the same time. This is not surprising, since both focus on demand creation and management: Keynesian economics at the macroeconomic level, the marketing principle at the microeconomic level.

In the early 1980s, as other economic theories replace to some extent Keynesian economics, we are witnessing also the replacement of the marketing principle with the resource management principle. This is no coincidence, since the focus of the resource management principle is on both supply and demand; thus it is better attuned to the economic reality that is facing us today.

There is one other important reason for the crisis of the marketing principle: most aspects of traditional marketing strategies have relied rather heavily on empirical approaches. As changes occur at an increasingly faster pace, experience becomes less and less relevant to the analysis of any contemporary problem. On the other hand, more quantitative approaches become increasingly important, to quantify the impact of risk and uncertainty, and to focus on better-defined concepts, such as profit and return on investment. The resource management principle can provide more practical answers in this kind of environment, since it is based on quantitative means to balance demand and supply, to optimize a given objective.

The Internationalization of Economic Activity. Long-term technological and political trends have set the stage for worldwide economic integration. In the early 1980s we can clearly see the beginnings of this process, which is being propelled by several factors, discussed in the following subsections.

Economic Maturity. As the U.S. economy continues its shift toward information-based activities, it is being followed by the other industrialized nations of the world. This trend intensifies the need for worldwide division of labor, or specialization, which is further encouraged by the need to profit from comparative advantages.

Comparative advantage considerations dictate the need to identify and use the most efficient local resources available at each place. Furthermore, this approach contributes to the solution of local sociopolitical problems: areas with high population and low income will tend to attract labor-intensive industries, to take advantage of labor supply and cost. This trend, in turn, will contribute to the solution of unemployment problems.

Economic Realignments. An increasing number of countries, such as Brazil, Mexico, South Korea, and Singapore, are becoming industrialized. At the same time, massive transfers of financial resources to some areas of the Middle East, Latin America, and Africa are setting the stage for significant, rapid, industrial development in those areas.

As a consequence, we can expect to see the emergence of important new supply sources for basic industrial goods such as petrochemicals, steel, pulp, automobiles, and light machinery. These new sources will be able to compete favorably with the older established industries in the industrialized countries, thus accelerating the process of international division of labor. In addition, as their economic development intensifies, the newly industrializing countries will be able to provide new additional markets for the more advanced products and for the services that industrialized countries can provide, thus further tightening the international economic web.

Worldwide Economic Integration. The availability of continuously improving means of communications and transportation is facilitating the economic process of worldwide economic integration. This is manifested by expanding trade agreements among larger and larger areas, such as the European Common Market and similar agreements in Latin America and Africa. Another important manifestation of this trend is the increasingly important work to simplify international trade practices and documentation.

Underlying all these factors is the need to obtain the greatest possible economies of scale in capital- and labor-intensive industries. In the late 1970s, it became clear that continental-size markets, such as the United States or Western Europe, are no longer sufficient to ensure the greatest possible economies of scale. This fact was clearly brought to the foreground by the success of the Japanese automotive industry and the failures of their American and European competitors.

An increasingly integrated world economy will see not only expanded markets but also additional—foreign—competition in the traditional markets of most industries.

Decreasing Self-sufficiency. During the 1970s it became apparent that there is no longer any possibility for a nation to be economically self-sufficient. Even the U.S. economy—traditionally the closest one to economic autarky—became irreversibly dependent on foreign trade. This point is

Table 2. *U.S. Imports of Selected Minerals and Metals as Fraction of Apparent Consumption*

Mineral	1960	1978	Differences (1978−1960)
Columbium	1.00	1.00	.00
Mica	.94	1.00	+.06
Strontium	1.00	1.00	.00
Manganese	.89	.98	+.09
Tantalum	.94	.97	+.03
Cobalt	.66	.97	+.31
Bauxite	.74	.93	+.19
Chromium	.85	.92	+.07
Platinum group	.82	.91	+.09
Asbestos	.94	.84	−.10
Fluorine	.48	.82	+.34
Tin	.82	.81	−.01
Nickel	.72	.77	+.05
Cadmium	.13	.66	+.53
Zinc	.46	.62	+.16
Potassium	—	.61	+.61
Selenium	.25	.61	+.36
Mercury	.25	.57	+.32
Gold	.56	.54	−.02
Tungsten	.32	.50	+.18
Antimony	.43	.48	+.05
Petroleum	.16	.47	+.31
Silver	.43	.41	−.02
Barium	.45	.40	−.05
Titanium	.22	.39	+.17
Gypsum	.75	.34	−.01
Iron ore	.18	.29	+.11
Vanadium	—	.27	+.27
Iron and steel	—	.13	+.13
Aluminum	—	.10	+.10

clearly illustrated by the information contained in Tables 2, 3, and 4 and Figures 13 and 14.

In Table 2 we see that there is a substantial number of raw materials being imported by the United States and that they represent a significant portion of U.S. consumption. Furthermore, we see that in most cases the relative importance of these imports is increasing, as evidenced by the difference shown between 1960 and 1978.

In Table 3 we see that the sources of supply of strategic raw materials to the United States are in a large number of countries spread out all over the globe.

Table 3.   *U.S. Major Foreign Sources of Selected Minerals and Metals, 1974–1977*

State	Minerals and metals
Algeria	Mercury
Australia	Bauxite, cadmium, zinc, titanium
Belgium	Cobalt, cadmium, zinc
Bolivia	Tin, tungsten, antimony
Brazil	Columbium, mica, manganese, tantalum, iron ore
Canada	Columbium, tantalum, asbestos, nickel, cadmium, zinc, potassium, selenium, mercury, gold, silver, tungsten, gypsum, iron ore, iron and steel, aluminum
Chile	Vanadium
China	Antimony
Dominican Republic	Gypsum
Finland	Cobalt
Gabon	Manganese
India	Mica
Indonesia	Tin
Ireland	Barium
Israel	Potassium
Jamaica	Bauxite, gypsum
Japan	Iron, steel
Liberia	Iron ore
Libya	Petroleum
Malagasy Republic	Mica
Malaysia	Tantalum, tin
Mexico	Strontium, fluorine, cadmium, zinc, selenium, mercury, silver, barium, gypsum
New Caledonia	Nickel
Nigeria	Petroleum
Norway	Nickel
Peru	Silver, barium

Table 3. (*continued*)

State	Minerals and metals
Saudi Arabia	Petroleum
South Africa	Vanadium, antimony, fluorine, asbestos, manganese, chromium, platinum
Spain	Strontium
Surinam	Bauxite
Switzerland	Gold
Thailand	Columbium, tantalum, tin, tungsten
Turkey	Chromium
Soviet Union	Chromium, platinum, gold, vanadium
United Kingdom	Platinum
Venezuela	Petroleum, iron ore
West Germany	Potassium
Yugoslavia	Selenium
Zaire	Cobalt
Zambia	Cobalt
Zimbabwe	Chromium

Table 4. *U.S. Exports and Imports as Fractions of GNP (Current Dollars in Billions)*[a]

Year	GNP ($)	Exports ($)	Exports Fraction of GNP	Imports ($)	Imports Fraction of GNP
1965	691.1	26.46	.0383	21.51	.0311
1966	756.0	29.31	.0388	25.49	.0337
1967	799.6	30.67	.0384	25.87	.0323
1968	873.4	33.63	.0385	32.99	.0378
1969	944.0	36.41	.0386	35.81	.0379
1970	992.7	42.47	.0428	39.87	.0402
1971	1,077.6	43.32	.0402	45.58	.0423
1972	1,185.9	49.38	.0416	55.80	.0471
1973	1,326.4	71.41	.0538	70.50	.0532
1974	1,434.2	98.31	.0685	103.65	.0723
1975	1,549.2	107.09	.0691	98.04	.0633
1976	1,718.0	114.75	.0668	124.05	.0722
1977	1,918.0	120.82	.0630	151.69	.0791
1978	2,156.1	142.05	.0659	175.81	.0815
1979	2,413.9	182.06	.0754	211.52	.0876
1980	2,627.4	221.97	.0845	248.71	.0947

[a] Source: Economic Report of the President (1981).

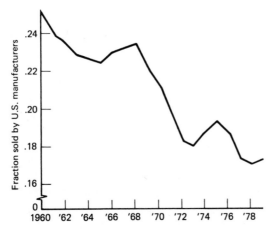

Figure 13. Manufacturing Exports of Industrial Nations. Source: U.S. Dept. of Commerce.

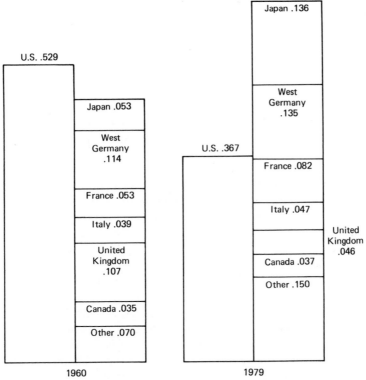

Figure 14. U.S. Share of World Output (Fraction of OECD Production). Source: U.S Dept. of Commerce.

In Table 4 we see that in only 15 years, U.S. foreign trade increased significantly: as a fraction of U.S. Gross National Product (GNP), exports have more than doubled, and imports have more than tripled. In 1965, foreign trade represented about .07 of U.S. GNP; by 1980, it represented about .18.

In Figure 13 we see that between 1960 and 1979 the U.S. fraction of world trade *fell* from .25 to .17. That is, despite a major increase in U.S. exports, they did not keep up with the explosive growth of world trade.

In Figure 14, we can see that between 1960 and 1979, the U.S. share of world output fell from .529 to .367, whereas the share of all major industrial countries, except the United Kingdom, grew.

The clear conclusions to be drawn from these figures are that even the U.S. has become a foreign-trade-dependent nation and that the dependency is increasing quickly. In the cases of all other nations, their dependency on foreign trade is greater than ours and is growing just as fast, or faster.

2.   THE RESOURCE MANAGEMENT CONCEPT

This concept can be viewed from two angles. It can be described in economic terms as the logical replacement to the marketing concept, as we have discussed before. It can also be described in operational terms as the result of progressive development in the management of physical resources. From this point of view, we can describe the resource management concept as the culmination of a series of historical stages that started with the first human groups.

As soon as the first human beings began to live in groups, they had to devise ways to transport and store goods—mainly food, and later clothing and tools. As larger groups gathered in the first cities and organized economic activities began to be characterized by the need to exchange goods, transportation of goods, by means of human or animal as well as wind-powered carriages and ships, took place both on land and water. At the same time, storage facilities emerged both to store grain for the cities and to store goods for merchants. These types of transportation and warehousing activities did not change much until the advent of the Industrial Revolution in England, toward the end of the eighteenth century. At that time, the invention of the steam engine gave birth to entirely new means of land and sea transportation: the railroads and steamboats that coexisted with animal-drawn carriages well into the twentieth century. At the beginning of the twentieth century, the practical application of the internal combustion engine saw the development of motor vehicles, and later on, airplanes. During the early part of this century, the internal combustion engine also began to change materials-handling methods; these had been based until then on the use of mechanisms such as wheelbarrows, dollies, and pulleys, which were in use for about 2000 years. Toward the end of the First World War motorized devices such as conveyors and small trucks started to become available for materials handling and warehousing. This state of affairs progressed throughout the 1920s and 1930s, with the increasing use of electric motors, which made it possible to handle increasingly heavier weights.

Throughout the twentieth century, the nature of economic activity changed drastically with the advent of mass-production techniques. Such techniques demanded the creation of large corporations capable of financing that type of production and of supporting the demand-creation activities that became grouped under the label of marketing.

During the Second World War, major advances took place in the area of military logistics, giving rise to major advances in materials handling, packaging, unitization, and transportation. Following the war, those techniques were applied to industry, giving rise to the concept of physical distribution.

2.1. Physical Distribution

The concept of physical distribution emerged from the application of the systems approach to the movement and storage of goods. For example, pallets and large containers to hold and transport them were designed so as to fit pallets snugly into the containers, to maximize cube utilization. At the same time, storage and handling devices were dimensioned to hold and move such pallets, and packages were dimensioned under the constraints imposed by the transportation, handling, and storage systems.

During the 1950s it became apparent that the physical activities just mentioned were also closely related to two types of information-processing activities: inventory control of finished goods and customer order processing. Thus, in the early 1960s the full concept of physical distribution was established and defined as encompassing all the activities needed to control, move, and store finished goods in their flow from the end of the production lines to the customers.

2.2. Logistics

During the 1950s and 1960s major cost reductions took place in the control, movement, and storage of finished goods through the application of the physical distribution concept. At the same time, other developments that took place during the Second World War evolved enough to provide additional opportunities to physical distribution practitioners. These developments took place in two areas: operations research and electronic data processing.

Operations research was born in Great Britain, in the 1930s, as an attempt to apply the methodology of scientific research to the solution of problems in military operations. Its two salient features were the use of multidisciplinary teams to study the different aspects of a given problem and the use of mathematical models as the main means of expressing the characteristics and relationships of all relevant parameters describing a given problem.

Electronic data processing originated in the United States in the 1940s with the creation of electronic machines capable of internally storing data as well as instructions to process that data. In the late 1950s, such machines became commercially available and started to displace electromechanical information-processing devices. First-generation computers, built with electronic tubes, were soon replaced in the early 1960s by second-generation computers, built with transistors, that provided expanded processing capacity and higher speeds, at lower unit costs. In the mid-1960s, third-generation computers, built with integrated circuits, started to replace second-generation machines, further enhancing their capability and reducing unit costs. In the early 1970s, new machines with large-scale integrated circuits furthered this process, which continued with the introduction of microprocessors, or computers-in-a-chip. These devices are changing the fashion in which automation is being applied to the economic process by making possible the construction of small, cheap, yet powerful computers that allow the dispersion of computer power into the hands of the ultimate users. Furthermore, microprocessors have quickly advanced the state of the art in process control and robotics.

While the developments in operations research and electronic data processing were taking place, parallel developments were occurring in manufacturing, transportation, and in materials-handling technology. The convergence of all these developments created the conditions, in the early 1970s, for the emergence of the logistics concept. The idea behind logistics was that all the techniques being used in physical distribution to control, move, and store finished goods could also be applied to similar problems affecting raw materials, components, and work in process, or unfinished products.

Furthermore, the availability of increasingly powerful, increasingly cheaper computers made it feasible to utilize operations research techniques of increasing complexity and power, in the design of decision support systems, to facilitate all aspects of material flow management. This circumstance enabled materials managers to expand the scope of their field even further to encompass within it the following functions:

Procurement, including sourcing, purchasing, warehousing, and inbound transportation of all materials needed by an organization.

Production planning, to translate sales forecasts into inventory requirements at given places and times, to be ready to ship on time. Production plans then serve as input to the production scheduling function.

Maintenance and replacement, including all the functions needed to procure, store, and dispense spare parts, tools, and manuals needed to maintain the products offered by an organization. In addition, this function encompassed the retrieval of products from customers for replacement.

Quality assurance, to ensure that all materials purchased or goods produced by the organization meet preestablished standards of performance or quality.

Recycling, of scrap, rejects, and by-products. This function became increasingly important as raw materials shortages became increasingly important.

Customer service, encompassing all relations with customers and prospects, except for direct sales and advertising.

The complete spectrum of functions described above, affecting all goods flowing into, through, and out of an organization, became the province of logistics. These functions are schematically shown in Figure 15, where it becomes apparent that logistics is the physical bridge between supply and demand markets.

It is important to note here that the successful integration of these functions under one overall major function was possible only through the use of increasingly powerful management systems, using operations-research techniques through effective automated data processing. The effect of the consolidation of all these functions was to expand the scope for cost trade-offs beyond that offered by physical distribution. The consequence was the attainment of increasing cost reductions and service improvements for organizations thus structured.

2.3. Physical Resource Management

The increasing application of operations research techniques and automated data processing to logistic operations not only enabled the emergence of the logistics concept but also made possible its expansion, which is currently under way, to a more general approach, which we will call physical resource management.

Physical resource management encompasses all logistic functions plus energy and real estate management. This concept crystalized in the early 1980s, as the culmination of several parallel developments:

The oil shortages that are precipitating a transition toward alternate sources of energy, as well as the need for more efficient energy procurement and management.

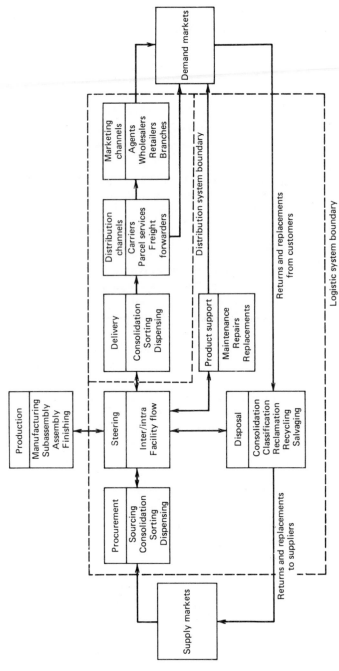

Figure 15. Logistic System Structure

The substantial increases in real estate prices throughout the world resulting from increasing urbanization to accommodate increasing populations. This factor has produced a situation where in many cases the land on which facilities are located has become more valuable than the facilities themselves. Thus, it is becoming increasingly important for all organizations not only to review more frequently their land portfolios but also to relate closely such analysis to the location of facilities and their financing.

The convergence of business data processing, process control, and telecommunications technologies. This circumstance enables the direct informational linkage between automated power plants and energy procurement systems, or between automated warehouses and inventory control systems, for example. Thus, it is possible to extend significantly, the scope of the system considered in order to obtain additional trade-offs and related economies.

2.4. Resource Management

Further technological advances are making it possible to structure physical resource management in the context of overall resource management in an organization. The main advances in this regard are:

The increasing use of microprocessors, which will enable organizations to provide individual computers to all personnel who need them. Such computers, with power comparable to the largest systems available in 1970, will be tied through communications links to all other such devices. They will provide local processing capabilities, data retrieval from archives, telephone and telegraph replacements, as well as more specialized features and access to large, remote processors.

Input–output devices will make substantial use of audio and visual technology, thus simplifying significantly the use of all processing devices.

As a result of these trends, it will become possible to integrate the work of large numbers of people of significantly different skill levels who are widely dispersed geographically. Thus, organizations will be structured around fewer, larger functions, and managers' span of control will be expanded.

The economic and technological trends we have discussed so far will result in a significant change in emphasis in the approach to organizational management: there will be a shift from functional orientation to a resource orientation. Such a shift will enable companies to cope successfully with the new economic environment by making use of the automation technology that is emerging. The manner in which this shift will take place and the basic technologies that will make it possible constitute the theme for the rest of this book.

2

The Resource Management Process

The resource management process is the set of all activities involved in the optimal allocation and administration of an organization's human, financial, and physical resources, through the application of its informational resources, to fulfill the organization's mission and achieve its goals and objectives.

This definition involves three interdependent processes:

1. *Directional thinking*, which is the process of defining an organization's mission, goals, and objectives.
2. *Resource allocation*, which is the process of allocating an organization's resources so as to optimize the value of an objective function.
3. *Resource administration*, which is the process of steering an organization's resources through their life cycles in the most efficient manner possible.

In the following section we will examine the characteristics of these three processes.

1. DIRECTIONAL THINKING

The thinking process can unfold in two distinct forms that alternate in a person's mind: structured thinking and creative or free thinking.

Structured thinking is mainly an analytic process; that is, it deals with a problem by breaking it down into components and examining the components and their relationships according to formal rules. This process may proceed through mathematical calculation, or through logical reasoning. In the latter case, it may proceed by deduction, applying general principles to draw conclusions pertinent to a component or relationship, or by induction, drawing general conclusions from observations of a few components, or relationships.

Creative thinking is mainly a process of synthesis; that is, it deals with a problem by focusing on any elements or properties that may be relevant to the problem, and by free association, structuring them into a solution to the overall problem.

Directional thinking is predominantly a creative thinking process. The objective of directional thinking is to arrive at a definition of the organization's mission, goals, and objectives. This process involves a fair amount of structured thinking, especially in the determination of objectives. However, it is important to emphasize that successful directional thinking is mainly a creative, free-thinking process, especially in formulating an organization's mission.

An organization's mission can be defined as the answer to the question, *What* should be the organization's business? This type of question cannot be effectively answered through the use of quantitative techniques, because too many important factors, such as the psychological impact of alternative answers on the organization's personnel and competitors, or the economic consequences of prevailing sociopolitical conditions, cannot be realistically quantified. By ignoring such factors, quantitative models describe only partial aspects of the question, and therefore the answers obtained from such models are usually incorrect.

It is the main role of an organization's top management to develop the answer to that question. Thus, the definition of an organization's mission is usually the result of its top managers' values, perceptions, and personal ambitions, rather than the result of objective calculations. However, management's thinking can be assisted by the use of structured techniques to comprehend, describe, and quantify parts of the total reality that must be dealt with. This is an iterative process, which finally establishes the organization's mission. It defines not only the scope of the organization's activities but also the state toward which the organization will move and the fashion in which the organization will integrate the needs of all protagonists with which it deals.

For example, an oil company may survey its position and redefine its mission as an energy company, or go further and redefine itself as a company in the natural resources business, or go even further and redefine itself as a company in the financial investment business. Each definition triggers a set of scenarios that detail alternative goals and objectives, and those, in turn, give rise to alternative strategies to meet such goals and objectives.

There are a number of unstructured thinking techniques that have been developed to guide and assist this type of process, such as brainstorming, synectics, and lateral thinking. However, in the end, the process depends mainly on the creativity and perceptions of the people involved in it.

The process of directional thinking consists of three steps: market segmentation, positioning study, and environmental study. Let us review those steps.

1.1. Market Segmentation

The first step in the directional thinking process is that in which the dimensions of the problem are identified by defining the set of options available to the organization. This is done by relating products and markets in a way that highlights where the organization is. and where it could go.

To accomplish the purposes of market segmentation, products and markets are usually consolidated into homogeneous groups. For example, products are usually consolidated along product lines with similar characteristics, such as performance, price, use, and service requirements. Demand markets are similarly consolidated according to meaningful similar characteristics, such as location, income, education, age, and life-style. In both cases—products and markets—the classification is further divided into existing and new products and markets.

Figure 16 shows a typical market segmentation matrix, in simplified form. In it, each product accounts for a row, and each market for a column. The intersections of rows and columns define cells, or market segments. The matrix in the example has four major regions, representing the different combinations between existing and new products and demand markets. Each region identifies a major possible strategic thrust for the organization, as follows:

The large square, representing existing products offered in existing markets, describes where the organization currently is and, therefore, the options associated with continuing as at present.

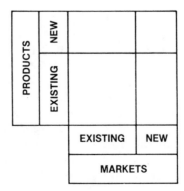

Figure 16.   Market Segmentation Matrix

The horizontal rectangle, representing new products that could be developed to supply existing demands, depicts a strategy driven by engineering and research and development considerations.

The vertical rectangle, representing existing products that could be offered to new markets, portrays a marketing driven strategy to develop new users for current products.

The small square, representing new products that could be developed and offered to new markets, shows the most drastic departure from current operations and requires the greatest strategic redeployment.

The last three regions identify the different new directions in which the organization may choose to go. In order to evaluate the desirability of the different alternatives identified, a positioning study is needed.

1.2. Positioning Study

A positioning study refines further the characteristics of each market segment in order to derive guidelines for strategic action.

In the last few years, many techniques have been proposed to provide generalized answers to positional problems. Some of the best-known techniques include the application of learning curves to determine the relative cost competitiveness of different organizations; the business portfolio approach, using, for example, a matrix relating the relative market share of an organization in a given market to the market's growth rate; the Profit Impact of Market Strategies (PIMS) approach, based on statistical correlations between different business parameters, such as sales volume and return on investment.

The results from the use of these techniques have been mixed. The reason seems to be that each concentrates only on certain aspects of the strategic problem. This simplifies the technique and its application but restricts its potential success to those situations where the few parameters considered are in reality the determining factors.

Our review of the existing literature leads us to conclude that many elements proposed in different techniques can be brought together in a synthesis that generalizes their scope. Thus, we can propose an approach to positioning that has enough generality to cope effectively with most situations commonly found in business by combining many features whose relevance has been identified in techniques of lesser scope.

The main conclusions that can be drawn from the analysis of different positioning approaches can be summarized as follows:

Successful strategies result from actions leading toward a predominant status in a market segment.

Problems result from failure to achieve or maintain a predominant status in a market segment.

Analysis of successful strategies indicates that there are four major variables that have determining influence on an organization's capability to achieve and maintain predominance. For a given market segment, they are delivered cost, market segment growth rate, net price, and performance differentiation.

Delivered Cost.   Delivered cost is the sum of all production and logistic costs needed to land products at a given market. The lower the delivered cost in a market segment, the greater will be the capability to achieve predominant status there.

Delivered cost is a result of the production technology used, and especially the adequacy of the degree of automation employed. It is also affected by the scale and scope of production operations and by the experience accumulated by the organization in the production of the products considered. The last point is usually described in terms of a "learning curve," relating the cumulative number of units that have been produced of a product to the time needed to produce the next unit. It has been found that there is a logarithmic relationship between those two variables, whereby typically a doubling of the number of units produced brings about a reduction in unit time of .15 to .20, with the consequent decrease in production cost.

The other factor that determines delivered cost is the logistic cost, involving the costs of controlling, moving, and storing raw materials, work in process, and finished goods, all the way to the demands. In many instances, unsuccessful strategies have been found to be the consequence of ignoring logistic costs and concentrating on production cost minimization alone. This is a serious mistake, because the lowest cost producer cannot necessarily deliver goods to the market at the lowest total cost. This situation is commonly found in companies that locate production facilities in areas with low labor and tax costs, for example, that prove to be too far from their demand markets, thus incurring significant penalties in transportation and warehousing.

The key to minimizing delivered cost is a well-designed logistic network, linking suppliers, production and logistic facilities, and customers by means of a transportation system. Such a network should be designed in a way that maximizes the difference between sales income and the sum of all costs needed to produce and deliver the products sold.

Market Segment Growth Rate.   This is the rate at which demand is growing in a given market segment. The growth rate is dependent on two major factors: environmental conditions and market segment age. Environmental conditions include the economic and political conditions under which the organization operates. These conditions are discussed at greater length in the subsection "Environmental Study," below. Market segment age is represented by the point at which the market segment is in its life cycle. The concept of market segment life cycle is illustrated in Figure 17.

When a product is offered to a market, the cumulative sales of that product, in that market, usually follow an S-shaped curve depicting the life cycle of that market segment. The market segment life cycle curve has three clearly defined segments:

1. *Introduction*, which is the period elapsed from the time the product is launched in that market until its sales takeoff, that is, until its sales growth rate starts growing at an accelerated rate.

2. *Expansion*, which is the period elapsed from the time of takeoff until the time of maturity, that is, when the sales growth rate starts growing at a decelerated rate.

3. *Saturation*, which is the period elapsed from the time of maturity until termination, which is the time when the product is withdrawn from that market segment and sales then cease.

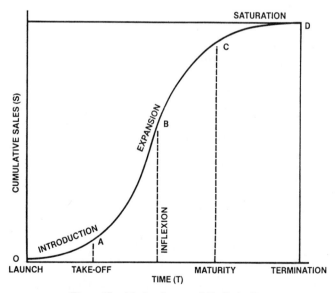

Figure 17. Market Segment Life Cycle Curve

Market growth rate is high during expansion and low during introduction and saturation. It is, however, critical to distinguish between low growth rates during introduction and during saturation, because they have major implications in the development of strategies. During introduction, a low growth rate is expected and tolerated because of expectations for future fast growth during expansion. Thus, activities in a market segment are terminated during introduction only when that period takes significantly longer than planned and it does not appear likely that expansion may be near. On the other hand, an unusually low growth rate at the saturation stage may by itself warrant withdrawal from the market segment.

This type of analysis may be formalized through the use of mathematical models. The life cycle curve can be described mathematically by the equation of a logistic curve, as

$$\frac{1}{S} = K + MN^T$$

or by a Gompertz curve, as

$$\log S = K - MN^T$$

In both cases:

$$T = \text{time elapsed}$$

$$S = \text{cumulative sales during } T$$

$$K, M, N = \text{constants calculated by regression}$$

Given an equation representing the market segment life cycle curve, the following definitions may be used for each segment:

Segment	Definition
Introduction	$\dfrac{dS}{dT} < 1$
Expansion	$\dfrac{dS}{dT} > 1$
Saturation	$\dfrac{dS}{dT} < 1$

And similarly, referring to Figure 17, we can define the intermediate points of greatest interest as follows:

Point	Definition
Take off (A)	$\dfrac{dS}{dT} = 1$
Maturity (C)	$\dfrac{dS}{dT} = 1$

The point of inflexion (B) where

$$\frac{d^2 S}{dT^2} = 0$$

is also a point of interest, because it defines the time at which cumulative sales start growing at a decreasing rate. Thus, even though growth rate is high at that time, its value starts declining after that point.

As a general rule, when the market segment growth rate for the period considered is .10 per year or more, in real terms, it is considered a high growth rate. However, the considerations stemming from the market segment's age should always temper the analysis.

Net Price. This price is that actually charged to customers, less all marketing expenses, less all applicable discounts. This is a relative measure, comparing the organization's price to those of its largest competitor at that market segment. As a rule, a relative net price of at least 1 is considered high. That would be the relative net price of an organization that has one of the highest net prices in a market segment.

Net price is determined mainly by discounts offered, the service provided, and the promotional efforts displayed for the market segment considered. However, other factors such as the uniqueness of the product or the existence of a captive portion of the market segment may also influence it.

Price and service decisions have traditionally been marketing decisions; they have been necessarily dependent or directly related not to costs but to competitive conditions and to intensity of demand. However, in a successful strategy, price and service—although not necessarily dependent on costs—should be related to costs, to ensure profit maximization given the assets available and the environmental conditions prevailing.

The relationship between price and demand is the well-known demand curve. That relationship, however, does not account for the influence of service on demand. Service can be measured from many different viewpoints. The most important measures are usually response time and order completeness. The relationship between demand at a market segment and price, response time, and order completeness is illustrated in Figure 18, where we

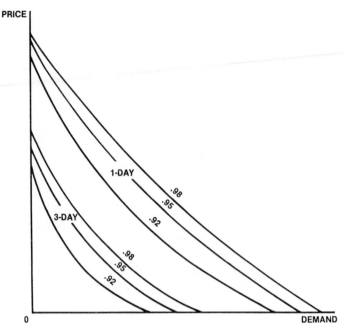

Figure 18. Expanded Demand Curve Concept

see one-day and three-day "demand bands," and within each band we can see curves for three levels of order completeness: .98, .95, and .92. Any one of those curves is in effect a classical demand curve with an implicit response time and order completeness. From those curves we can see that a given demand can be attained by many different combinations of prices and service characteristics.

Furthermore, each demand band corresponds to a given level of promotional effort. Additional promotion tends to "move" the demand bands upward and rightward, and vice versa. Expanded demand curves can be developed using marketing research techniques and conjoint analysis, or they can be simply estimated on the basis of prior experience.

In assessing relative net price for the future period considered in the positioning study, it is therefore necessary to bring into the analysis all the parameters just discussed. On that basis, an estimate can be made as to whether expected relative net price will be high or low for the market segment considered.

Performance Differentiation. This is the degree of uniqueness that the product offered has with regard to competitive products offered in the market considered. Uniqueness is mainly a function of the product's appearance, its performance, and the service backup offered. Appearance is dictated by product design; performance, by design, by production methods, and by quality standards and assurance methods used in its production. Service backup is dependent on the quality of the customer service system available to maintain the product in working order.

In a positioning study it is necessary to classify performance differentiation. This is usually done through a combination of market research and testing. Market research techniques are useful in establishing how a product's design compares with those of the competition. They are also useful in determining the perceptions of customers in relation to product performance and service support.

Product performance can be measured further through testing of competitive products. However, it is important to note that customer perceptions about performance are more important than tested performance, since customer perceptions—right or wrong—determine their actions. Performance differentiation is considered high when the product's performance, appearance, and service support are perceived as at least equal to those of any other competitor.

The fashion in which the four variables just described interact in a positioning study depends on their relative importance in the market segment considered. Often, predominant status in a market segment is achieved or maintained most profitably when the following conditions are present with the following priority:

1. Low delivered cost
2. High market segment growth rate
3. Low net price
4. High performance differentiation

Market segments exhibiting all these characteristics can be expected to yield significant profits, while at the same time achieving or maintaining predominance. At the other end of the spectrum, market segments with all the opposite characteristics are clear candidates for elimination. Other market segments, exhibiting some of the characteristics above, require further positioning study.

A useful way to show all the strategic alternatives stemming from the different combinations of market segment conditions is to plot them in a tree, as shown in Figure 19. This tree is plotted so that the different combinations of conditions are displayed in a typical descending order of desirability. The best combination is at the top, showing low delivered cost, high market

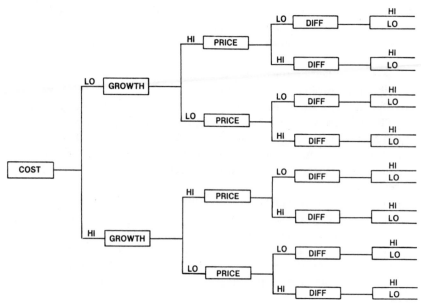

Figure 19. Positioning Study Tree

segment growth rate, low net price, and high performance differentiation. The worst combination is at the bottom, showing the exact opposite characteristics. The two extreme conditions mentioned give rise to rather obvious guidelines for the allocation of resources to them. In the case of most favorable conditions, it is clearly a question of allocating the necessary resource to maintain or improve such conditions. In the other extreme case, it is normally desirable to terminate participation in the market segment.

The most complex situations are those between the two extremes, because there are no general rules to guide the allocation of resources to them. These are the situations that require the greatest creativity on the part of management to ensure that the right amount of resources are allocated to them and that they are used for the right purposes.

Although it would be too lengthy to outline general courses of action for each of the remaining 14 possibilities, it is worthwhile to discuss some intermediate cases to illustrate the ideas discussed here. For the sake of clarity, we will use a modification of a well-known technique and array some of the most interesting combinations of factors in the positioning study matrix shown in Figure 20. There we see that market segments with the best possible combination of factors are designated as "Tigers," and those with the worst possible combination of factors as "Dinosaurs." The two intermediate cases

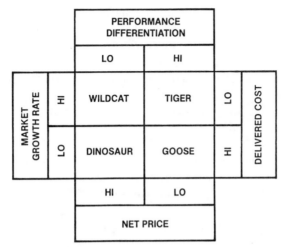

Figure 20. Positioning Study Matrix

shown in Figure 20 are designated as "Wildcat" and as "Goose"; each case has two favorable and two unfavorable factors.

In the case of a Wildcat, representing a market segment with high market growth rate and low delivered cost, but with high net price and low performance differentiation, it is normally advisable to allocate to it enough resources to decrease its net price and increase its performance differentiation and try to convert it into a Tiger. In the case of a Goose, representing a market segment with low relative net price and high performance differentiation, but within a market showing low growth rate and having a high delivered cost, it is normally advisable to allocate to it just enough resources to keep it going and to transfer income from it to Tigers and Wildcats. Under certain conditions, however, it may be desirable to allocate to it the necessary resources to lower its delivered cost and make it a more desirable market segment to keep for the long run.

1.3. Environmental Study

The third step in the directional thinking process, environmental study, is often conducted in parallel with the other two. Its purpose is to describe and assess the overall context in which the organization must operate to support the activities of a given market segment. An environmental study deals with two types of factors: particular and general. The main particular factors affecting the profitability of a market segment are:

Competition to be confronted in that market segment, their strengths and weaknesses as perceived by the market, and an evaluation of their likely reactions toward different competitive strategies.

Supply conditions, including the availability, reliability, and expected prices of the resources needed to produce and deliver the products to the demands considered.

Regulations, affecting the costs, types of processes that can be used, and, in some cases, product design characteristics.

The most important general factors affecting the profitability of a market segment are several types of conditions expected to prevail at the places where products are to be produced, transformed, and delivered, including:

Social conditions, such as the general level of satisfaction with political and economic conditions, the adequacy of social services available, and the degree of identification with common goals.

Political conditions, such as the existing institutions of government and their expected stability and the legal framework in existence.

Economic conditions, such as the availability of resources, tax conditions, financial incentives, levels of employment, inflation rate, and extent of freedom for capital flows.

Technological conditions, such as the efficiency of the production processes.

Environmental factors serve to guide market segmentation and positioning studies. Furthermore, these factors are usually decisive in making final commitments of resources to any market segment. By their nature, they are usually hard to quantify, therefore they place the greatest demands on management's ability to think creatively and balance perceived risks and uncertainty.

At the beginning of our discussion on directional thinking, we defined an organization's mission as the answer to the question, *What* should be the organization's business? From our discussion, we can conclude that another output of such process is a statement of goals. An organization's goals can be defined as the answer to the question, *Why* should the organization pursue a given mission? The answer to such a question is formulated in terms of marketing goals—such as increasing market share—financial goals—such as increasing return on equity—and social goals—such as increasing employment opportunities.

In Chapter 1, we discussed at some length the general environmental factors that are likely to affect business conditions in the coming years. In this chapter, we have discussed how those conditions are brought into the management process as part of directional thinking. We have seen how directional thinking leads to the identification of organizational mission and goals and sets the stage for the establishment of specific objectives. In more specific terms, the directional thinking process defines the specific market segments that an organization should consider in evolving its strategy. In addition, it provides basic information about each market segment, such as expected demand curves, costs of entering or staying in each market segment, and constraints and conditions that may have to be observed because of environmental or internal reasons. In effect, directional thinking identifies the niches in the business environment in which the organization may fit well in the future, their major characteristics, and their overall requirements.

The next step in the resource management process is to allocate the resources available to the organization among the competing market segments. That is the purpose of the resource allocation process.

2. RESOURCE ALLOCATION

Resource allocation is the distribution of scarce, versatile resources to satisfy multiple ranked requirements in a way that optimizes benefit. Examining this definition, we see that four conditions must exist *simultaneously* to create a resource allocation problem:

Scarcity of resources; that is, the availability of each resource is insufficient to meet all stated requirements.

Versatility of resources; that is, the possibility of using any one resource available to satisfy more than one requirement.

Multiplicity of requirements; that is, the need to satisfy more than one requirement.

Ranking of requirements according to some criteria that establishes relative desirability.

The definition also refers to optimizing benefit. In that context, benefit can be measured as profit, cost, throughput, time, or employment level, for example. Optimizing refers to maximizing or minimizing a given benefit.

The resource allocation process provides the answers to the questions, *When, where,* and *how much* resources will be allocated? The answers to those questions become the organization's objectives. Thus, objectives are the result of management's calculations, not the point of departure for developing strategies.

Objectives are always numerically stated and have a time frame attached. For example, an objective may be to attain a 14% market share in a given market segment by the end of 1985.

To proceed with the resource allocation process, it is necessary to define, for each market segment, the following parameters:

1. *Strategic direction*, specifying whether the market segment should be expanded, maintained, contracted, or abandoned.

2. *Demand characteristics*, including the forecast demand by customer or geographic area as a function of price, service, and promotional intensity. Forecast demand is usually broken down at each area to reflect expected ordering characteristics, such as the distribution of order sizes, and service quality. Furthermore, minimum quantities that must be delivered and maximum quantities not to be exceeded are defined.

3. *Supply characteristics*, including the location of each supplier of raw materials and other purchased items, their price structure, including discounts and minimum quantities, and maximum quantities to be purchased from any one supplier or location.

4. *Facility characteristics*, including for each existing and potential facility its location, its mission—production or logistic operations—all costs involved, material balance equations relating the amounts of inbound materials needed for each unit of outbound product, minimum and maximum capacity acceptable, plus any other practical conditions that may have to be respected in the production or logistic processes.

5. *Financial conditions*, such as total capital available for investment and operations, hurdle rate of return to be used, inventory carrying cost, depreciation schedules, and replacement policies.

6. *Overall conditions* that must be met when allocating resources, in order to account for contractual obligations, personnel agreements, engineering conditions, and others.

7. *An objective* to be met by the allocation of resources. This may be profit maximization, cost minimization, throughput maximization, service maximization, for example, or a combination of such factors.

Let us now examine the characteristics of data describing these parameters and some of the problems usually encountered in practice to develop such data.

2.1. Resource Allocation Data

Any organization that allocates resources by some method has the necessary information to do so. The most typical problem with resource allocation data is not their availability but their accuracy.

When an organization allocates resources by informal means, some of the data are estimated or implicity assumed. Furthermore, in many organizations the only systematically developed data are accounting data; such data are usually developed to comply with legal and auditing requirements. As is the case with most data developed in transaction processing systems, they are not adequate to support the decision-making process. The main reasons for this are described in the following subsections.

Different Objectives. Transaction processing systems, such as accounting systems, are concerned with record keeping, variance measuring, tax considerations, and risk minimization, for example. Decision support systems, such as resource management systems, are concerned with representing the real world in a reasonably accurate way. For example, depreciation of assets is treated in a totally different way in each type of system.

In an accounting system, depreciation is normally calculated so as to amortize as much of the original cost as soon as possible. The purpose is to create the maximum cash flow allowed by law and to minimize risk. Thus, the annual amortization figures shown in accounting books have no necessary relationship to the physical, actual depreciation of the asset.

In a decision support system, typically an amortization charge will be calculated by transforming the actual expected amortization stream into an equivalent payment series that represents the asset's expected life and deterioration, instead. In some instances, when evaluating the replacement of assets, their replacement values instead of book values may be used. Although different organizations follow different policies, the important point is that in a decision support system the data used can have a significantly different value than the equivalent data in a transaction processing system. Despite such differences, both sets of data may be correct for the purposes for which they were developed.

Different Basis. Transaction processing systems use costs based on arbitrary definitions—such as fixed, semivariable, and variable costs—that contain arbitrary cost allocations—such as overhead—and implicit assumptions—such as given capacity utilization rates or product mixes.

Decision support systems require cost structures that avoid arbitrary definitions, allocations, and assumptions, because such arbitrary bases are normally calculated as part of the decision under examination; therefore, they must not be assumed a priori. For example, in determining a production standard cost, the usual practice will be to assume a given capacity utilization and product mix, and through allocations of overhead, energy, and indirect labor, a standard is established, that contains fixed and variable portions.

On the other hand, in a decision support system, a production standard cost will be arrived at by first developing cost equations relating production levels to different cost elements, then finding the optimal production level and adopting that cost as the standard.

The data used in resource allocation are expressed in terms of three basic units and combinations of them. The basic units are those that measure *physical* magnitudes, such as weight or volume, *time*, and *money*. Examples of such units are tons, days, and dollars. Derived units contain two or all three types of basic units. Examples of derived units are cents per hundredweight, pounds per day, and dollars per ton per year.

For a given time period, there are three types of resource allocation–related data: costs, constraints, and conditions. Let us examine these types of data from a problem-solving point of view in the following subsections.

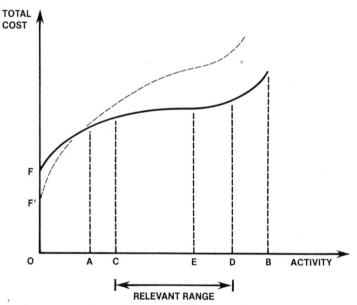

Figure 21. Operational Cost Structure

Costs.   Usually one considers total rather than unit costs, and they are expressed as a function of physical or time units, by means of cost equations. A typical operational cost equation can be plotted, as shown in Figure 21. There we see a relationship between the level of activity at a facility or process, or piece of equipment, and the total cost resulting from it. The level of activity may be measured as throughput weight and/or volume, and/or time elapsed.

In Figure 21, there are several points of interest along the cost relationship. There is a cost intercept, such as F, that represents the cost associated to the asset when its activity is zero. There are two points representing physical limits within which activity takes place; these are a minimum (A) and a maximum (B) level of activity. The minimum level of a process is usually determined by such factors as inertia, friction, and air or other fluid's resistance. In a facility, its minimum activity level is usually determined by minimum operational conditions, such as the minimum size crew needed. The maximum level of a process or facility is usually determined by physical limitations: it is that capacity obtained by operating the asset at maximum speed, 24 hours per day, 365 days per year.

In addition, there are operating minimum (C) and maximum (D) activity levels, dictated by good engineering practices, contractual obligations, or economic conditions. The range between C and D is usually known as the relevant range. This is the range within which asset activity normally takes place.

Furthermore, in any production or logistic process, there is an optimal point (E) where the unit cost is minimal; this is usually the design activity level of the asset. As the activity level increases, economies of scale allow total cost to increase at a decreasing rate up to E. Beyond that point, diseconomies of scale set in, and total cost starts increasing at an increasing rate.

The cost intercept (F) is the point where the cost relationship intersects the cost axis: it provides the right cost scale. As the asset ages, the total cost relationship shifts upward, to positions such as that shown in the broken line curve starting at F'.

From a decision-making point of view, all costs must be considered variable; that is, they are always a function of the asset's activity level. When the activity level reaches the maximum value, additional investment can create additional capacity; this may be in the form of expanded or new facilities, or accelerated or additional equipment. In some instances, additional investment is desirable for economic reasons, before the maximum is reached.

Such conditions are illustrated in Figure 22, where we see that as activity in the facility or process considered increases, the operational cost curve just described takes place, starting from point F, at activity O, and going to the

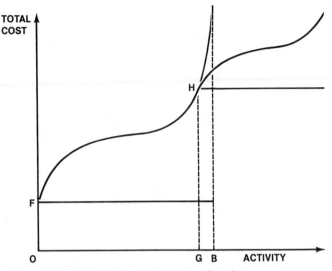

Figure 22.   Decision-Oriented Cost Structure

maximum B. In Figure 22, we see that before B is reached, at a level such as G, it is more economical to increase the investment in the asset up to a point such as H, in order to expand capacity and lower total costs beyond G.

From Figure 22 we can see that the total cost structure is the sum of two types of costs:

Discontinuous costs, which vary stepwise, such as those shown at activity levels O and G and beyond. These costs can be operational, such as the intercept cost (F), or can be special, lump-sum costs, such as closing-down, disposal, and changeover costs.

Continuous costs, which vary at every level of activity. These may include direct raw materials and energy costs, for example.

We have previously pointed out that decision support data must be structured in a way that avoids a priori assumptions about the solution being searched. In allocating resources, it is essential to observe that principle. An efficient way to avoid arbitrary, a priori cost allocations is to define operational costs as a tree structure. Thus, continuous and discontinuous costs can be described in relation to facilities, processes, and products.

Figure 23 shows a typical cost tree structure. In it, we see facility-related, process-related, and product-related costs. Every cost relationship is developed by itself, relating activity levels to total cost, without allocating any costs. Since the cost relationships are described by equations, it is not necessary to select any particular set of conditions to arrive at cost figures.

The cost equations shown in Figure 23 form a tree structure because they are related to one another by the condition that all costs are added at every branching point. Thus, all product-related costs are added to their common process costs, and all process-related costs are added to their facility-related costs.

Since accounting data are not a good source of decision support data, such data must be developed independently. The two most common approaches to develop decision support costs are:

Engineered costs, developed by costing out an engineering description of process behavior.

Regression costs, developed by fitting a curve to a sample of observations.

In both cases, the greatest accuracy is needed for points within the relevant range.

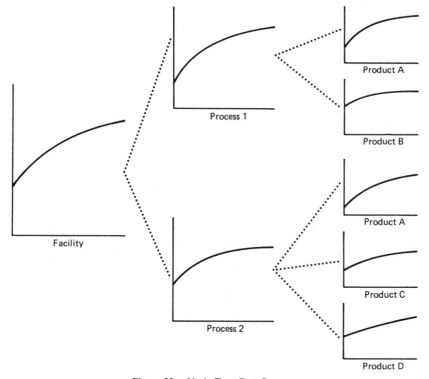

Figure 23. Node Tree Cost Structure

Constraints. Constraints are numerically expressed characteristics that must be respected in developing the optimal allocation of resources. They usually reflect physical limitations or targets inherent to the situation considered. Typically, constraints are maximum and minimum values of activities within which the solution must lie—the limits defining the relevant range, for example. Other types of constraints are usually expressed as ratios among resources: for example, material balance equations relating quantities of inbound raw materials to outbound finished goods, at a production facility or process.

Conditions. Conditions are logical, nonnumeric characteristics that must be respected in developing the optimal allocation of resources. They usually reflect business considerations, such as policies, contractual obligations, or customer service needs.

Conditions can be described in terms of expressions involving logical operators, such as:

If–then/else
And
Or
Not/nor

Examples of conditions found in practical resource allocation problems are: "Every customer should receive products B and C from the same shipping location as product A." "If product 1 is made in machine X, then product 2 should not be made in that machine but should be made in either machine Y or Z." "If project I is funded, then project Q must also be funded."

2.2. Resource Allocation Technology

The technology needed to perform true allocation of resources was developed in the late 1940s. Then George Dantzig's technique for optimizing linear programs was published. However, that technology had only limited applications for about 20 years. In the 1960s, with the advent of large, fast, low-cost computers, it became practical to use any of a variety of optimization techniques that are designated by the general label of mathematical programming to solve practical resource allocation problems effectively.

Before the practical diffusion of mathematical programming techniques, resource allocation problems were handled with heuristic approaches. Because of their simplicity, such approaches have lingered on, and even in the early 1980s there are still occasional references to them. For this reason, we will briefly discuss here the basic characteristics of heuristic techniques.

Essentially, a heuristic approach to a problem is a systematic form of trial and error. When the number of possible alternatives is so small that they can be easily enumerated, a heuristic approach may be practical because it is possible to cost out all possible alternatives and identify the one that maximizes benefit.

In most real-life situations, enumeration is not feasible; therefore, heuristic techniques cannot provide an optimal answer, or even an estimate of it. This is a serious limitation for several reasons:

Since optimal solutions are not guaranteed, it is impossible to guarantee that resources have been allocated in a way that maximizes benefit. Thus, heuristic methods almost always offer an inferior solution that wastes resources. Furthermore, lack of an optimal solution means lack of a meaningful benchmark to allow the rational evaluation of quasi-optimal alternatives.

A heuristic approach is a reflection of its author's intuitive feelings about the structure of a "good" solution. Thus, heuristic methods are bound to arrive consistently at solutions of a predetermined nature. The technique does not offer the potential for skill transferring that enables the identification of counterintuitive solutions.

Lack of optimality makes it impossible to conduct meaningful sensitivity analysis, to establish the impact on the solution of potential errors in the input. Under conditions of increasing uncertainty, this limitation can lead to extremely inefficient solutions that must be corrected at great expense, thus increasing the inefficiency of the heuristic approach. By the same token, marginal analysis becomes impossible under nonoptimal conditions.

Given these limitations, and considering the high cost-effectiveness of mathematical programming techniques that can be implemented with the aid of computers, this type of analysis has rendered heuristic approaches obsolete for solving any serious resource allocation problems. Thus, our discussion of resource allocation technology will revolve around the different types of mathematical programming techniques available for this purpose. These techniques include linear programming, integer programming, dynamic programming, and nonlinear programming. We will review the basic ideas behind these techniques in the remainder of this section. However, before we do so, it is useful to place them in perspective by first outlining two earlier developments in optimization theory that set the background for the development of mathematical programming techniques. These two developments are the theory of optimization of continuous functions, which stemmed from differential calculus, and the method of Lagrange Multipliers, which solves particular cases. Throughout this discussion, we will assume that the reader is already familiar with the basic concepts of differential calculus.

Optimization of Continuous Functions.   Given a continuous function Y of an independent variable X, such as shown in Figure 24, we can identify a number of points of interest in the interval IJ; we have A, showing the higher or global maximum, B a local minimum, C a local maximum, D a point of inflexion, where the function passes from positive to negative curvature without acquiring an extreme value, and E the lowest or global minimum. If the function is described by an equation of the type $Y = f(X)$, it can be demonstrated that whenever the condition

$$\frac{dY}{dX} = 0$$

exists, there is an extreme point—maximum or minimum—or a point of inflexion. Furthermore, if in addition the condition

$$\frac{d^2Y}{dX^2} \neq 0$$

is also satisfied, then the point represents a local minimum, if the value of the second derivative is positive, or a local maximum if it is negative. If its value

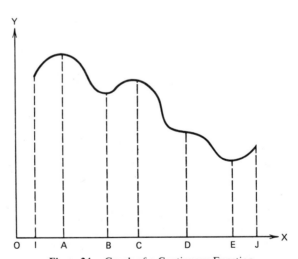

Figure 24.   Graph of a Continuous Function

is 0, further analysis is needed to establish whether there is an extreme value or a point of inflexion. If all the points having extreme values in the interval IJ have been identified, then the highest local maximum and the lowest local minimum are the global extremes in that interval.

To illustrate this principle, let us examine a typical allocation problem. If regression analysis indicates that there is a good relationship between sales (S) and advertising expenditures (A) in a given market segment for values of A between 100 and 1,000 (thousands of dollars), represented by the equation

$$S = 580 + 1.4A - .001A^2$$

it is necessary to find the optimum level of advertising expenditures. To that effect, we find the value of A such that

$$\frac{dS}{dA} = 0$$

thus, we have:

$$\frac{dS}{dA} = 1.4 - .002A = 0$$

therefore: $A = 700$. And since

$$\frac{d^2S}{dA^2} = -.002$$

is always negative, we can conclude that sales will be maximized when advertising expenditures equal exactly 700; at that level, sales will be 1,070. Any other level of advertising, higher or lower, will result in lower sales. Since the value found is within the range considered, we can also be sure that we have found the global maximum.

When more than one independent variable is necessary to define a function, similar procedures are followed, partially differentiating the dependent variable with respect to each independent variable, one at a time (holding all other independent variables constant), setting all the resulting equations equal to 0, and solving the system of simultaneous equations. Thus, to find the optimum value of $Y = f(X_1, X_2, X_3, \ldots, X_n)$ we would set

$$\frac{\partial Y}{\partial X_1} = 0$$

$$\frac{\partial Y}{\partial X_2} = 0$$

$$\vdots$$

$$\frac{\partial Y}{\partial X_n} = 0$$

and the solution to that set of simultaneous equations would yield the values of the X_i that optimize Y.

Lagrange Multipliers.   In the preceding example, we saw that the optimum value sought fell within the range of validity of the original function. Thus, despite that the relationship between sales and advertising expenditures was valid only for values of A between 100 and 1,000, that constraint was not brought explicitly into the calculations. If the optimum value found would have fallen outside the valid range, then the closest value to it within the range would have been chosen as the best solution under the circumstances.

We can see that when a simple constraint must be considered in the process of finding an optimal answer, it is easy to do so. However, in many practical situations things are not so simple. When a function must be optimized subject to a set of constraints, and/or the nature of the constraints is rather complex, we need a technique powerful enough to match the complexity of the problem. Such technique is known as the technique of Lagrange Multipliers. Although a proof of its validity is beyond the scope of this book, we will outline here the basic principles behind the technique.

The general problem can be stated as follows: Optimize $Y = f(X_1, X_2, X_3, \ldots, X_n)$ subject to the following constraints:

$$g_1 (X_1, X_2, X_3, \ldots, X_n) = 0$$
$$g_2 (X_1, X_2, X_3, \ldots, X_n) = 0$$

$$\vdots$$

$$g_m (X_1, X_2, X_3, \ldots, X_n) = 0$$

To find the optimal solution, we proceed as follows: A new function Y_λ is created such that:

$$Y_\lambda = f(X_i) + \lambda_1 g_1(X_i) + \lambda_2 g_2(X_i) + \ldots + \lambda_m g_m(X_i)$$

where the coefficients λ_i are known as Lagrange Multipliers. Then we set:

$$\frac{\partial Y_\lambda}{\partial X_1} = 0$$

$$\frac{\partial Y_\lambda}{\partial X_2} = 0$$

$$\vdots$$

$$\frac{\partial Y_\lambda}{\partial X_n} = 0$$

$$\frac{\partial Y_\lambda}{\partial \lambda_1} = 0$$

$$\vdots$$

$$\frac{\partial Y_\lambda}{\partial \lambda_m} = 0$$

The solution to that set of simultaneous equations provides the values of the variables X_i that optimize Y subject to all constraints.

To illustrate the technique, let us go back to our previous example and assume that a more accurate relationship has been found between advertising level and sales. The new relationship, however, is also a function of the expenditure in customer service (C) and is defined by the equation

$$S = 125 + 2.3A - .0015A^2 + .9C$$

We are required to find the values of A and C that will maximize S. However, the solution must meet one practical constraint: our budget allows a maximum of \$950,000 for both advertising and customer service, thus:

$$A + C = 950$$

is a constraint that must be respected to arrive at a practical answer.

Following the procedure outlined before, we set a new function, as follows:

$$S_\lambda = 125 + 2.3A - .0015A^2 + .9C + \lambda(A + C - 950)$$

and we set the partial derivatives of S_λ with respect to each of the variables equal to 0:

$$\frac{\partial S_\lambda}{\partial A} = 2.3 - .003A + \lambda = 0$$

$$\frac{\partial S_\lambda}{\partial C} = .9 + \lambda = 0$$

$$\frac{\partial S_\lambda}{\partial \lambda} = A + C - 950 = 0$$

From that system of simultaneous equations we can calculate the values of A, C, and λ, and we have:

$$A = 466.67$$
$$C = 483.33$$
$$\lambda = -.9$$

The values found of A and C maximize S subject to the constraint that their sum must be 950. Under those conditions, $S = 1306.67$.

Linear Programming.   We applied the method of Lagrangian Multipliers to a typical practical problem and obtained a solution that allocated resources in a way that maximized a given function. However, that was possible only because the constraint was described by an equality. If some or all of the constraints are described by inequalities, then the technique of Lagrange Multipliers does not apply, and we must use even more powerful tools to find the optimal allocation of resources. The simplest of such tools is linear programming; it is also one of the most widely used tools in management science.

The adjective *linear* is used to state that all the mathematical relationships used in formulating a linear programming problem must be linear; that is, the exponent of all variables must be 1. *Programming* is meant in the sense of planning or strategy development. A problem can be stated in terms of a linear programming formulation when it meets all of the conditions enumerated in the following discussion.

There is an "objective function" that must be optimized. The objective function may be a cost, profit, sales, or production level, or any other magnitude whose maximum or minimum value is sought.

There is a set of independent variables or "activities." The independent variables, or activities, are interrelated. Their main interrelationship expresses the objective function. Additional interrelationships express constraints in the problem.

There is a set of "constraints" that must be respected. Constraints are different interrelationships among sets of activities. These are expressed in terms of inequalities, although some of them may be equalities. Constraints are expressed in terms of a relationship between activities, usually written on the left-hand side of the inequality, and a constant, or limit, that must be exceeded (minimum) or cannot be exceeded (maximum). The value of the constant is usually written on the right-hand side of the inequality. The optimum value of the objective function must be such that the values of all activities that produce the optimum also meet all the constraints defining the problem.

All variables must be expressed numerically, be known with certainty, and be linear. The objective function and all constraints must represent magnitudes that can be expressed as numbers with positive or zero value. Their values must be known with certainty and must all be continuous and linear; that is, their exponents must be 1. They cannot appear in expressions containing products of two or more variables.

As a consequence of this latter condition, in all linear programming problems both the objective function and the constraints are polynomial expressions in which each term can be expressed as the product of a numeric coefficient and a variable of degree 1. Furthermore, the solution may contain fractional values for some variables.

To illustrate these characteristics, let us consider a simple resource allocation problem, which we will solve using linear programming. A company has $20 million that must be invested in any of four projects designated as Projects A, B, C, and D. The expected returns on investment are as follows:

Project	Return
A	.12
B	.14
C	.16
D	.18

However, because of the risks involved in different projects, the following limits have been placed on the investments that can be allocated to the projects:

The investment in Project D should not exceed $5 million.

The investment in Project B should not exceed $8 million.

The sum of the investments in Project B and C should not exceed $10 million.

The investment in Project A is limited only by the total amount available for investment.

We need to determine how much should be invested in each project in order to maximize the total return on investment, while at the same time meeting all the constraints established for the projects.

Let us express this problem in mathematical terms, as a linear programming problem. Defining:

$$A = \text{amount to be invested in Project A}$$

$$B = \text{amount to be invested in Project B}$$

$$C = \text{amount to be invested in Project C}$$

$$D = \text{amount to be invested in Project D}$$

$$Z = \text{total return on investment}$$

we can express the objective function as:

$$Z = .12A + .14B + .16C + .18D$$

We need to find the values of $A, B, C,$ and D that will maximize Z, subject to the following constraints:

$$A + B + C + D = 20$$
$$B \leq 8$$
$$B + C \leq 10$$
$$D \leq 5$$

To solve this problem, we will use an algorithm known as the Simplex method. An algorithm is a method of calculation that has an initial step, an iteration procedure that converges toward a final solution, and a testing procedure to establish that the final solution has been obtained. To use the Simplex method, we will first transform all the constraints into a system of simultaneous equations. Since most of the constraints are inequalities, they can be transformed into equations by introducing "slack variables," as follows:

$$A + B + C + D = 20 \qquad (1)$$

$$B + S_1 = 8 \qquad (2)$$

$$B + C + S_2 = 10 \qquad (3)$$

$$D + S_3 = 5 \qquad (4)$$

The slack variables S_1, S_2, and S_3 are added to the left-hand side of the inequalities when their sign is $\leq$, and subtracted when their sign is $\geq$.

The system of simultaneous equations constituted by the objective function and Equations (1) through (4) are usually displayed in matrix form, assigning a column to every variable and a row to every constraint equation. Extracting the coefficients from those equations, a detached coefficient matrix is defined. In our example, it appears as follows:

A	B	C	D	S_1	S_2	S_3	RHS
.12	.14	.16	.18	0	0	0	Z
1	1	1	1	0	0	0	20
0	1	0	0	1	0	0	8
0	1	1	0	0	1	0	10
0	0	0	1	0	0	1	5

There is a column for each variable (A, B, C, D, S_1, S_2, S_3) plus one more column representing the right-hand side (RHS) of each equation; the RHSs are the limits constraining the problem. The rows represent the coefficients of each variable in the objective function and in Equations (1) through (4).

It can be seen that the majority of the elements of the detached coefficient matrix are 0s. This is a usual situation; it is common to define the "density" of the matrix as the ratio between the number of nonzero coefficients and the total number of coefficients.

Continuing with our problem, we now have a system of four simultaneous equations with seven variables (A, B, C, D, S_1, S_2, S_3). To solve this problem, we apply the procedure described in the following paragraphs.

First, we find any solution involving four variables only (the same as the number of equations) that meets all the constraints of the problem. Such a solution is called an initial or feasible solution. In our case, we will start with the following solution:

$$A = 5$$
$$B = 8$$
$$C = 2$$
$$D = 5$$

which implies $S_1 = S_2 = S_3 = 0$. This solution respects all the constraints, therefore it is a feasible solution. The nonzero variables A, B, C, and D are called basic variables, and the set of four variables is known as a basic solution or basis. The variables set to 0 are known as nonbasic variables. The total return from this basic solution is:

$$Z = .12 \times 5 + .14 \times 8 + .16 \times 2 + .18 \times 5$$

or

$$Z = 2.94$$

Next, we need to determine whether this is an optimal answer, and if not, how to improve on it. To this effect, we proceed as follows: we express all the basic variables in terms of non-basic variables. Thus, from Equations (1), (2), (3), and (4) we obtain:

$$A = 5 + S_3 + S_2 \tag{5}$$
$$B = 8 - S_1 \tag{6}$$
$$C = 2 - S_2 + S_1 \tag{7}$$
$$D = 5 - S_3 \tag{8}$$

and replacing these values in the objective function

$$Z = .60 + .12S_3 + .12S_2 + 1.12 - .14S_1 + .32$$
$$- .16S_2 + .16S_1 + .90 - .18S_3$$

or

$$Z = 2.94 - .06S_3 - .04S_2 + .02S_1$$

We see that the constant term 2.94 is the value of the total return for this solution, as we found before.

Examining the equation above, we determine whether this is an optimal solution. We see that of the three terms containing nonbasic variables, there is one term that is positive: $.02S_1$. This indicates that if the value of S_1 were increased above its current value of 0, the value of Z would increase. Thus, we can conclude that this is not an optimal solution and therefore that it can be improved.

To improve on the solution, we examine all the positive terms in the equation and select the one that has the largest coefficient. In our example, the only positive term is S_1; therefore, we select it for further analysis.

Next, we introduce S_1 into the basis and force one of the current basic variables out of it. This is accomplished by clearing S_1 from one of Equations (5) through (8). There, we find that S_1 appears in Equations (6) and (7). To select which equation to clear S_1 from, we need to determine in which equation is the value of S_1 constrained most.

In Equation (6) we see that S_1 could increase up to the value 8. Beyond that value, it would force B to be negative, which is not acceptable in a linear programming formulation. In Equation (7) we see that since S_1 has a positive sign, it can increase indefinitely without forcing C to be negative; the only constraint here is the condition that C could never be greater than 10.

We will then pick Equation (6) to clear S_1. Thus, we have:

$$S_1 = 8 - B$$

and replacing this value in Equations (5) through (8), we obtain a new basis:

$$S_1 = 8 - B \tag{9}$$

$$A = 5 + S_3 + S_2 \tag{10}$$

$$C = 10 - S_2 - B \tag{11}$$

$$D = 5 - S_3 \tag{12}$$

We now repeat the iterative procedure and replace these values in the objective function, obtaining

$$Z = .60 + .12S_3 + .12S_2 + 1.6 + 16S_2$$
$$- .16B + .90 - .18S_3$$

or

$$Z = 3.10 - .06S_3 - .04S_2 - .16B$$

We can see that the value of the objective function has increased to 3.10; furthermore, we see that there are no positive terms in the last equation defining Z. Therefore, we can conclude that no further improvement is possible and that we have found the optimum answer.

The optimum answer is derived from Equations (9) through (12), where the nonbasic variables are 0, and, therefore, the values of the basic variables are:

$$S_1 = 8$$
$$A = 5$$
$$C = 10$$
$$D = 5$$

The fact that the slack variable S_1 has a value of 8 implies from Equation (2) that B must be 0. Thus, the optimal solution is:

$$A = 5$$
$$B = 0$$
$$C = 10$$
$$D = 5$$

which maximizes profit while respecting all constraints.

The fact that linear programming guarantees an optimal solution for a given set of feasible conditions is its major attraction. This feature not only leads the decision maker toward strategies that provide the highest possible benefit but also provides a "benchmark" against which alternatives can be measured. Since any alternative containing more constraints than the original problem will by definition be suboptimal, linear programming models enable the calculation of the penalties associated with nonoptimal solutions. Thus, the decision maker can choose between following an optimal strategy, or paying a known penalty and following a nonoptimal one.

Furthermore, a linear programming formulation provides a framework for conducting several types of analyses of the behavior of the problem and its solution under varying conditions. This is a major requirement for a management system to cope successfully with uncertainty. Let us briefly review these ideas.

When the optimal answer has been identified, managers still need to answer many questions about the impact that errors in demand and cost forecasts, or in the assumed values of constraints, for example, would have on the optimal solution. Furthermore, managers need to gain a deeper understanding of the behavior of the system and the solution, in order to perceive clearly *why* the optimal answer is the best solution. For example, it is necessary to understand how much more profit could be made if some constraints were moderately relaxed.

Linear programming, as well as all other optimizing resource allocation techniques we will discuss, enables the user to gain such understanding. This is another major reason for using optimization techniques to allocate resources.

The deeper understanding about the behaviors of the system and the solution comes from analyzing the sensitivity of the system and the solution to changes in input values. This "sensitivity analysis" can take many forms, which are described in the following subsections.

Marginal Analysis. In the example discussed above, we found that the optimal solution indicated that Project B should not be funded—despite that its expected return was higher than that of Project A. The reason for such results is the existence of constraints, limiting the resources that could be devoted to different projects, as well as in total.

An important question for managers is, How much difference would it make if some constraints were changed? Going back to our problem, the question can be stated in more precise terms as, How much would the total return increase if a given right-hand side were increased by one unit, allowing one million more to be invested in that particular project? Determining the answer to that type of question is the subject of marginal analysis.

We define marginal value as the variation effected in the objective function by a change of one unit in a given right-hand-side value. Given an optimal solution, it is easy to calculate the marginal value for each right-hand side. These values provide a guideline for which constraints may be of interest to change; that is, the highest marginal value for a solution would indicate the constraint that it may be most useful to relax. The statement just made was worded in a conditional fashion because the conclusions derived from marginal analysis are valid only within limits. The limits are imposed by the basis: the marginal value of a constraint is valid only as long as the variation in the value of the right-hand side *does not change the basis*.

A similar analysis can be performed with the coefficients in the left-hand side of the constraints. There we find coefficients affecting two kinds of variables: structural variables—those that define the objective function— and slack variables.

If we examine a structural variable, marginal analysis will enable us to determine the rate of change in the objective function if a variable that is not in the basis were introduced in it. This analysis indicates the amount by which either the cost is too high or the profit is too low to make it desirable to introduce the variable into the basis. This information can be used to guide pricing and cost reduction actions.

If we examine a slack variable, marginal analysis will enable us to determine the rate of change in the objective function with respect to changes in resource availabilities or requirements. This rate of change is sometimes known as a "shadow price."

Shadow prices can be especially useful in establishing transfer prices. This is so because shadow prices represent the rate of change of the objective function for marginally higher or lower activity levels representing flows between two entities in the problem.

Ranging Analysis. This technique deals with the evaluation of the impact on the value of the objective function stemming from changes in values in the terms included in the objective function. Thus, we can calculate the *range* within which an activity can vary—such as the magnitude of investment in a given project—or within which a coefficient can vary—such as a profit margin or cost—without changing the structure of the optimal answer.

Ranging information is useful because it allows managers to assess how much a level of activity, a cost, or a profit margin can change without altering the structure of the optimal solution. Conclusions derived from a given range are valid only when all other parameters in the objective function are kept constant and when the variation is within limits that do not change the basis.

Another interesting piece of information that can be derived from ranging analysis is that of reduced cost or profit. This is the magnitude of the change needed in a nonbasic variable to make it part of the basis. For example, it could indicate how much more demand a product must have to make it profitable to include it in the solution.

Parametric Analysis. The two preceding techniques depend on input changes made one at a time, and only within a range that does not change the basis. When it is important to establish the consequences of simultaneous changes in any set of parameters in the detached coefficient matrix, within or without their validity range, we deal with parametric analysis.

Although the discussion of the techniques available to perform systematically parametric analysis is beyond the scope of this book, it is important to mention because it is a useful feature normally available in standard computerized linear programming programs. The basic idea behind parametric analysis is that when a new strategy is being developed, it is indispensable to go beyond the determination of the optimal answer for the original set of parameters that defined the problem. It is necessary to assess the validity of such parameters and the impact of simultaneous changes in them on the solution.

Simultaneous changes may affect any terms in the matrix: in the right- or left-hand side, or in the objective function. For example, if we wish to study the effect of changing the right-hand sides, each right-hand-side coefficient can be assigned a rate of change (positive, negative, or zero), and then a parameter is defined that varies continuously from 0, in such a way that:

New RHS = old RHS + (parameter $\times$ rate of change)

Each row in the matrix may be given a different rate of change, but the parameter is always given the same value for all rows. Thus, as the parameter varies, it reflects the simultaneous changes in all right-hand sides.

Recursive Analysis. This technique is an extension of parametric analysis. That analysis reflects the changes in the solution resulting from simultaneous changes in a set of inputs. After each calculation of this type, a new calculation can be made varying new parameters; the new parameters to vary are chosen on the basis of the results previously obtained.

When general rules to perform successive parametric analysis runs are introduced, they constitute recursive analysis. This type of analysis is normally automated and is embedded in the linear programming program. Recursive analysis is then a convenient way to expedite the performance of parametric analysis.

Reverberation Analysis. We have seen in marginal and ranging analysis how the impact on the objective function could be assessed, as a function of changes in the values of the right-hand sides, or of the terms in the objective function. We can extend this type of analysis to encompass the effect of changes in right-hand-side or objective-function terms, both on the value of the objective function and on the values of the basic variables. For instance, if the value of the maximum investment allowed in Project D would increase—or decrease—by one unit, we could determine the impact of such change on total return and also on the values of the investments to be made in the other projects.

The variations in the values of the objective function as well as of the basic variables are expressed as substitution rates, which are calculated by varying one term at a time in the right-hand side or in the objective function.

Another form of reverberation analysis is to determine the effect of changes in left-hand-side terms on both the objective function and the basic variables. This type of change will usually be associated with changes in process technology; such changes, upgrading the efficiency of the process, would be translated in different values for the left-hand-side coefficients. This type of analysis allows the decision maker to identify the improvement magnitude that may be needed from technological enhancements in order to increase the profitability of the system.

The variations in the values of the objective function as well as on the basic variables, are expressed as upgrading rates. These are calculated by varying one left-hand-side coefficient at a time, within its validity range.

Quasi-Optimal Analysis. The five major techniques outlined in the preceding sections take advantage of the structure of a linear programming problem to derive useful information from its optimal solution. Quasi-optimal analysis takes advantage of the fact that a linear programming formulation always yields an optimal answer to a feasible problem.

The idea behind quasi-optimal analysis is that the optimal solution may be only slightly better than other solutions that may be simpler in structure or easier to implement and manage. Thus, it is of interest to find quasi-optimal solutions, that is, solutions whose objective function value is only slightly worse than that of the optimal solution. The difference between the values of the optimal and the quasi-optimal objective functions is known as the penalty.

To illustrate this concept, let us solve graphically a two-dimensional linear programming problem, stated as follows: a company sells two products, designated as A and B; the profit margins are $3 per unit for product A, and $7 per unit for product B. Both products are manufactured using three machines, which we will designate as M_1, M_2, and M_3, so that to make one unit of product A it is necessary to use 2 hours of M_1 plus 1 hour of M_2, plus 5 hours of M_3. To make one unit of product B, it is necessary to use 1 hour of M_1 plus 3 hours of M_2, plus 6 hours of M_3. In the planning period considered, machine availabilities are 40 hours for M_1, 60 hours for M_2, and 150 hours for M_3. We are required to find the quantities of A and B that should be produced to maximize profit, while at the same time meeting the constraints imposed by machine availability.

Let us state the problem mathematically. If *A* and *B* denote the quantities of respective products to be made, then we have the following objective function

$$Z = 3A + 7B$$

and the constraints on machine time availability can be stated as

$$M_1: 2A + B \leq 40$$

$$M_2: A + 3B \leq 60$$

$$M_3: 5A + 6B \leq 50$$

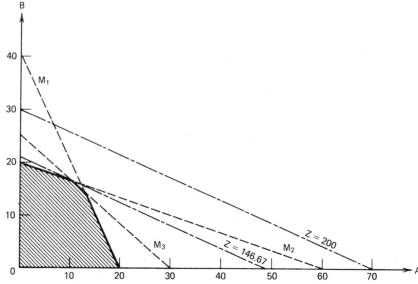

Figure 25. Graphic Solution to a Linear Programming Problem

In order to solve the problem graphically, as shown in Figure 25, we start by plotting the constraint inequalities. This is done by plotting the lines representing the limit, or equality conditions. Thus, we can plot $2A + B = 40$ and obtain line M_1 in the graph, and, similarly, we can obtain lines M_2 and M_3.

Each line defines a region between itself and the pair of axis, that is, the region containing all points that meet the constraint established by the inequality. When the three lines M_1, M_2, and M_3 are plotted, they define an area within which all points meet all constraints. Such area is shown shaded in Figure 25 and is known as the feasible region.

The next step is to find which point within the feasible region represents the optimal—or maximum profit—solution. To this effect, we plot the objective function for an arbitrary value, such as $Z = 200$, shown in Figure 25, as a dash-dab line, so labeled. We see that $Z = 200$ lies outside the feasible region; this means that the optimal solution will yield a total profit lower than 200. If we were to draw successive lines for lower values of Z, they would be parallel to $Z = 200$ and would get progressively closer to the feasible region. The line that would touch the feasible region would be the one representing the value of the optimal solution. The coordinates of the point of contact define the values of the optimal activity levels.

In the example, the line representing $Z = 146.67$ touches the feasible region at the point $A = 10$, $B = 16.67$. Thus, we can see that the optimal solution calls for 10 units of product A and 16.67 units of product B and that this solution will yield a maximum profit of $146.67.

We can now perform quasi-optimal analysis on the optimal solution. This takes the form of establishing an acceptable penalty, such as .05 of the optimal objective function. Under these conditions, any solution yielding a profit between $146.67 and .95 of it, or $139.33, would be considered acceptable.

Going back to the graphic solution, we can draw the feasible region at a larger scale, as shown in Figure 26. We can then draw the optimal objective function, represented by the line $Z = 146.67$, and the lowest acceptable objective function, represented by the line $Z = 139.33$. The last line will intersect the feasible region, creating an acceptable region—shown shaded in Figure 26. The acceptable region contains all the points representing quasi-optimal solutions within the acceptable penalty. Thus, we can choose any point in the acceptable region, such as P, and its coordinates will represent the activity levels of an acceptable quasi-optimal solution. In the case of P, we have $A = 8$ and $B = 17$. Under these conditions, $Z = 143$, which is .98 of the optimal solution, and therefore within the acceptable penalty.

Quasi-optimal analysis is of great importance in the development of strategies for large-scale systems, such as large logistic, production, or financial systems. A major reason is that the optimal solution may be only slightly

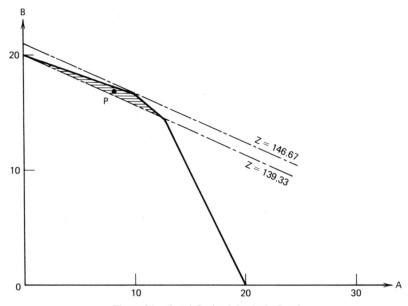

Figure 26.   Quasi-Optimal Analysis Graph

better than several quasi-optimal solutions with acceptable penalty. However, equally important is that quasi-optimal analysis also enables a manager to study the full impact of trade-offs between different cost elements in the system, as well as between costs and service levels.

That optimization models can be used to evaluate quasi-optimal solutions in a systematic, controlled fashion also means that managers can use such an approach to assess if their original problem statement was formulated in the most effective manner. Thus, the analysis of quasi-optimal solutions may lead to a restatement of the original problem in a fashion that reflects more adequately the real dimensions of the situation under consideration.

The preceding discussion of the characteristics of the linear programming technique and the advantages of using optimizing techniques gives an overall idea of the power of this type of decision support technique. However, despite its power, linear programming has several important limitations. These are the consequences of all the conditions that a problem must meet to be susceptible to a linear programming formulation and solution. We will now discuss additional mathematical programming techniques that have been developed to deal with particular limitations of linear programming.

Goal Programming. One of the major characteristics of a linear programming problem is that it requires the optimization of a single objective function. In many real-life problems, this type of formulation is not realistic, as the decision maker must strive to attain several objectives at the same time. Under those conditions, the problem is to get as close as possible to all the objectives stated, while trying to respect as much as possible the constraints established.

Goal programming is a technique to deal with this type of problem. The approach is to define all the objective functions that characterize the problem and to establish for each a value or *goal* that it would be desirable to attain. Then, each objective function is assigned a weight, representing its relative priority or importance. The solution to the goal-programming problem is the compromise that minimizes the weighted sum of all the deviations between the goals and the values attained for their respective objective functions.

For example, if we have two objective functions for the decision variables A and B, and we establish goals for each, we would have:

$$Z_1: a_1A + b_1B = g_1$$
$$Z_2: a_2A + b_2B = g_2$$

where a_i and b_i are coefficients, and g_i goals. If both objective functions have the same weight, then we can define a composite objective function

$$Z = |(a_1A + b_1B - g_1) + (a_2A + b_2B - g_2)|$$

that we wish to minimize. The vertical lines around the right-hand side signify the absolute value of the expression within.

To minimize Z, we can transform the problem into a linear programming problem as follows: first, we define a set of auxiliary variables representing the deviations from goal for each objective function.

$$d_1 = a_1A + b_1B - g_1$$
$$d_2 = a_2A + b_2B - g_2$$

Since the deviations d_i can be positive or negative, we can express their absolute values as a sum of two types of positive variables: a positive deviation, and a negative deviation, or;

$$d_1 = d_1^+ - d_1^- \text{ therefore } |d_1| = d_1^+ + d_1^-$$

and

$$d_2 = d_2^+ - d_2^- \text{ therefore } |d_2| = d_2^+ + d_2^-$$

so that the problem becomes one of minimizing

$$Z = d_1^+ + d_1^- + d_2^+ + d_2^-$$

subject to the constraints

$$a_1A + b_1B - (d_1^+ - d_1^-) = g_1$$
$$a_2A + b_2B - (d_2^+ - d_2^-) = g_2$$

which is a typical linear programming formulation.

The goals assigned to objectives will not necessarily be met: they may be exceeded or unattained. For this reason, goal programming is not truly an optimizing technique but a *satisficing* technique. It attempts to satisfy as closely as possible the goals established, without guaranteeing that they can all be exactly met.

Integer Programming.   The greatest limitation of linear programming in practical problems is its requirement that all variables be linear. This means, for example, that a production cost must be described as a linear function of the quantity produced. This condition is seldom realistic. Typically, production costs will have a lump—or fixed—cost that is independent of the quantity produced, and then, total cost will increase at a decreasing rate because of economies of scale, up to a point, beyond which costs increase at an increasing rate because of diseconomies of scale. Furthermore, in some problems, some of the components considered are potential not actual; for example, in a problem, some facilities considered may be potential facilities being explored. In those cases, their costs would be incurred only if the facilities were called for in the solution; otherwise, neither their fixed nor their variable costs would actually be incurred. None of these characteristics can be modeled using linear programming.

In addition, in many practical problems, solutions containing fractional values are not realistic. For example, a company producing airplanes cannot manufacture 3.4 airplanes of a given model. If fractional answers from a linear programming solution are rounded, the resulting solution will seldom be the optimal solution for integer values, and in many cases, it may not even be a feasible solution.

All of the problems outlined above can be solved by an extension of linear programming, known as integer programming, or a variety of it, known as mixed integer programming, in which only some variables must have integer values. A description of the solution algorithm for mixed integer programming problems is beyond our scope. However, it is useful to point out that this type of problem can be solved with commercially available software and that the formulation guarantees a global optimum answer.

The main problem with mixed integer formulations is that they require substantially more computation time than linear programming. However, as computers become faster and cheaper, this feature becomes decreasingly important. Mixed integer programming has proven to be an extremely powerful tool to model highly complex problems in a realistic fashion. Thus, the solutions provided by this type of model are extremely practical.

Other Mathematical Programming Techniques. Although linear programming and mixed integer programming are by far the most commonly used optimizing resource allocation techniques, several other techniques have been found useful under particular circumstances. The main ones are described in the following subsections.

Dynamic Programming. This is an approach to solving certain types of problems, not a technique such as linear programming. It is an approach to solving problems that require an optimal strategy, under conditions where it is necessary to make a time-sequenced set of interrelated decisions. The main characteristics of a dynamic programming problem are:

The total problem is divided into two or more stages, sequenced in time. At each stage, multiple alternatives are available.

At each stage, a decision is needed, and the decision taken at each stage associates that stage to the next one.

Given any stage, the optimal policy covering all subsequent stages is not dependent on the decisions made at previous stages.

A typical example of a dynamic programming problem is that of scheduling production operations to meet seasonal demands without accumulating too much inventory and maintaining employment within predetermined levels so as to minimize cost.

An important variation of dynamic programming is probabilistic dynamic programming, in which at any stage the states for the next stage are not fully known but can be described in terms of the probabilities associated with the occurrence of each state. This type of problem is commonly known as a decision tree.

Nonlinear Programming.   In discussing mixed integer programming, we pointed out that the technique can be used to handle nonlinear relationships, such as costs containing economies of scale. This is accomplished by approximating the nonlinear function by means of a polygon. Thus, mixed integer programming introduces a slight inaccuracy in the formulation, although such inaccuracy can be kept as low as desired by increasing the number of sides of the polygon used, as discussed in Appendix B.

Under special conditions, nonlinear relationships can be handled directly, without a polygonal approximation. That is the approach known as nonlinear programming. For example, techniques known as quadratic programming can be used to optimize a quadratic objective function (that is, one that contains second-degree variables), subject to linear constraints.

The techniques involved in nonlinear programming are beyond the scope of this book, but it is important to mention them despite their limited practical application to date. Significant research is currently being conducted in this area and will be greatly helped by increasingly cost-effective computers. As these techniques become more powerful, they will provide an increasing level of fidelity to mathematical models.

2.3. Resource Allocation Effectiveness

After a resource allocation strategy has been developed and implemented, it is important to measure to what extent it was actually followed and how close the actual results were from those predicted. We will call such a measure the effectiveness of the resource allocation process.

A simple definition of resource allocation effectiveness can be established by focusing on the value of the objective function optimized. Thus, by comparing the actual value obtained in practice with the calculated value arrived at in the optimization calculation, we have a measure of how close to optimal was actual performance.

Thus, if we define:

E = resource allocation effectiveness

A = actual value obtained for the objective function

C = calculated optimum value for the objective function

we have:

$$E = \frac{A}{C}$$

The value of E measures how well the resources were actually allocated. From a somewhat different point of view, E measures the extent to which the resources available were used for the right purposes.

3. RESOURCE ADMINISTRATION

The administration of resources is the part of resource management that deals with two basic questions:

How should the organization's resources be utilized to fulfill its mission and achieve its goals and objectives?

Who should be responsible for making what decisions and taking what actions to cope with internal and external events and their outcomes?

To answer those questions, it is useful to look at the life cycle of each resource and to the processes that must be performed to guide an organization's resources through their life cycles.

3.1. Resource Life Cycle

The processes that constitute a resource life cycle are illustrated in Figure 27. They fall under one of two major categories: stewardship or execution.

The processes within stewardship are planning and control; these processes are interactive in the sense that the planning process produces objec-

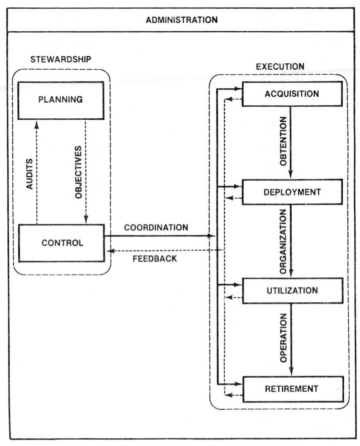

Figure 27.   Resource Life Cycle Processes

tives to guide the control process, and the control process culminates in audits of the execution processes that serve, in turn, to guide subsequent planning. An important conclusion from this description is that both planning and control are dynamic, continuous processes that are constantly interactive in order to be successful. In effect, whenever one becomes a static, occasional undertaking, this is a symptom of poor stewardship. Control, in turn, triggers and steers the execution processes, providing coordination and receiving feedback from them.

The direction set by the stewardship processes is translated into action through four sequential execution processes. The first is acquisition, which transforms the plans for allocated resources into a procurement strategy to obtain the necessary resources. Once resources are obtained, they must be deployed and organized to become useful. At that stage, resources can be utilized through the operation of physical, human, financial, and informational systems. Finally, resources must be retired from the system, closing the life cycle of the resource. We will review in more detail the characteristics of each one of these processes in the following subsections.

Planning. The first step in resource administration is to convert the resource levels allocated for different purposes into coherent, specific plans of action, detailing how and when the organization should proceed to acquire, deploy, utilize, and retire such resources. Planning is usually conducted at three interrelated levels, with different time horizons and at different levels of detail. The shorter the time horizon, the higher is the level of detail. Typically, we can define strategic planning as covering a period starting 2 or 3 years in the future and reaching 10 or more years in the future. Tactical planning covers a period starting 1 year in the future and reaches 2 to 3 years in the future. Operational planning covers the year ahead. The major characteristics of planning systems are summarized in the following subsections.

Strategic Planning. The main thrust of strategic planning is to define options to be opened, retained, and closed regarding the market segments of interest to the organization and their consequent financial and operational consequences. This takes the form of identifying which market segments to invest in, which ones to dispose of, and which ones to continue at a low level of investment.

Strategic planning has an external orientation, dealing mainly with long-term trends of a demographic, social, political, economic, and technological nature and with their implications—threats and opportunities—for the future of the organization. The planning horizon is divided into irregular periods typically of one-, two-, and five-year durations.

The main inputs into the strategic planning process are scenarios that are considered worthwhile to explore and forecasts that describe the best assessments of important developments. Its main outputs are policies, constraints, and conditions that govern tactical and operational planning.

Tactical Planning. The main thrust of tactical planning is to define the resources needed and their purposes, quantities, and timing. It deals with external factors, including competition, regulation, and supply, and with internal factors, such as the availability of managerial personnel and limits on the availability of other resources.

The planning horizon is usually divided into quarterly increments. The main inputs into the tactical planning process are forecasts and projections based on past trends. Its main outputs are assessments and decisions to guide operations.

Projections are statistical extrapolations of past trends described as time series. They are produced using a variety of techniques, such as regression, multiple correlation, or the Box–Jenkins approach. Forecasts may use projections as an input but in addition will use econometric analysis, marketing research information, and management's assessment of the impact of environmental factors on the organization's performance. Generally, projections are not reliable beyond a couple of years. Forecasts are seldom reliable beyond about five years. Furthermore, both techniques require several years of history to make their calculations significant.

Operational Planning. The thrust of operational planning is to define how to use the resources that are available. It deals with internal factors: sequencing and scheduling operations and translating such plans into instructions for executions and budgets. The planning horizon is usually divided into monthly, weekly, and daily increments. When operational plans become part of automated process control, they may be described in real-time terms.

The main inputs to operational planning are customer orders and projections. Its main outputs are recommended actions and reactions to environmental outcomes, in order to guide the execution processes.

As the nature of planning gets more strategic, it requires increasingly creative thinking, and as it gets more operational, it requires increasingly structured thinking. However, the resource allocation technology discussed previously can be effectively used at all levels: at the strategic level, to provide support by enhancing and expediting the assessment of alternatives; at the operational level, by automating most of the process and thus providing skill transferring and amplification.

A major consideration in the planning process is that it should be viewed as an integrating process. That is, planning at all levels should be all-encompassing from both a functional and a resource standpoint. Thus, marketing, financial, and production plans, as well as facilities, equipment, and materials plans, for example, should all be aspects of the same single overall plan; this ensures compatibility and integration of all aims.

Another major consideration affecting the planning process is that it should be participatory; that is, it should represent the ideas of as many people as possible. This ensures that the objectives established by the planning process are widely shared and are perceived as a good representation of individual aims. With increasing uncertainty and complexity, the planning process is more important than the plan itself.

Control. The control process is exercised in a similar fashion at all levels of planning and for all resources involved. In every instance, control is exercised in two directions: feedback and coordination.

Feedback takes place in three steps. First, it *measures* actual performance, expressed in terms analogous to those of the plan. Second, it *compares* actual performance against the plan and calculates the deviation from it. Third, it *identifies* the corrective actions needed to eliminate the deviations. Coordination, in turn, triggers the corrective actions needed to steer the organization back to the planned course.

At the strategic level, control deals primarily with checks on the validity of the assumptions concerning demographic, social, political, technological, and economic trends and their impact on the organization. Typically, strategic control is exercised semiannually or annually.

At the tactical level, control deals with checks on the validity of assumptions concerning competition, regulation, and supply and with the validity of forecasts and projections. Furthermore, at this level control deals with identifying opportunistic actions that may provide unplanned advantages. Typically, tactical control is exercised monthly or quarterly.

At the operational level, control deals with reactions to changes in orders and projections, and with the exploitation of short term advantages that were not planned. Typically, operational control is exercised in very short intervals, or in real time.

Furthermore, the control process interacts with the planning process by providing audits from execution feedback, receiving revised objectives from planning, and using them to guide subsequent coordination.

Acquisition. The first of the execution processes is acquisition. It takes the objectives and directions established by the stewardship processes, identifies the necessary actions to acquire all the resources needed to support the plans, and includes the performance of such actions. Acquisition results in the obtention of the resources required. This information is fed back to the control process, with specification of whether all resources needed have been obtained. If some resources are not obtainable, changes in plans may result in order to adapt objectives to availabilities.

Acquisition of resources can take place in a variety of forms for different resources, including:

Physical resources, through purchase, lease, rental, extraction, or growth.

Financial resources, through borrowing or collection.

Human resources, through recruiting and hiring.

Informational resources, through data collection.

Deployment.   Once resources have been acquired, they must be deployed. This takes the form of organizing and placing all resources in a fashion that renders them useful.

Deployment of resources can take place in a variety of forms for different resources, including:

Physical resources, through building of facilities, installation of equipment, and dispersion and storage of inventories.

Financial resources, through the establishment of credit lines.

Human resources, through structuring an organization and training.

Informational resources, through the structuring of data bases or of files.

Utilization.   After resources have been deployed, they can be utilized to fulfill the organization's mission and attain its goals and objectives.

Utilization of resources can take place in a variety of forms for different resources, including:

Physical resources, through producing, converting, growing, transporting, storing, and maintaining.

Financial resources, through payments and exchanges.

Human resources, through motivation and direction.

Informational resources, through the transmission, storage, retrieval, and processing of data.

Retirement.   At some time during the utilization of resources, they become depleted or reach a state in which no further utilization is necessary, possible, or desirable. At that point, resources are retired from the organization and are no longer available to it.

Retirement of resources can take place in a variety of forms for different resources, including:

Physical resources, through sales.

Financial resources, through liquidation or long-term commitments.

Human resources, through termination or retirement.

Informational resources, through the display or issuance of outputs.

3.2.   Resource Administration Technology

Resource administration deals with decision making and action taking to cope with the outcomes of environmental events. The key to efficient resource administration is the ability to make correct decisions under different states of knowledge of the environment.

The states of knowledge of the environment can be described in terms of a spectrum, varying from complete certainty to complete ignorance about the possible outcomes of an event. Thus, it is useful to classify the conditions under which decision making must take place into four categories, discussed in the following subsections.

Certainty. Certainty is the characteristic of events such that all their possible outcomes are known, and, in addition, the one outcome that will take place is also known. These circumstances, rather unusual in practice, present no major problem in arriving at a correct decision.

Ignorance. Ignorance is the characteristic of events such that none of their possible outcomes are known. Under these conditions, no rules can be established to guide the actions of the decision maker.

Uncertainty. Uncertainty is the characteristic of events such that some, but not all, their possible outcomes are known, and such that it is not possible to estimate the probability that any given outcome will take place.

As we discussed earlier, coping with uncertainty requires management systems that provide:

Adaptability, that is, the ability to maintain or improve performance under changing, uncontrollable circumstances.

Skill amplification, that is, the ability to enhance human performance through systems that provide increased speed, flexibility, accuracy, and consistency.

Contingency planning, that is, the ability to anticipate major changes and provide potential responses to them in a prompt, well-structured, complete fashion. These are some of the characteristics of automated decision support systems, which we will discuss in later sections.

In addition, coping with uncertainty requires the accumulation of resource reserves to enable an organization to cope with unexpected problems and exploit unexpected opportunities. Faced with uncertainty, a decision maker can proceed either by making some nonquantitative assumption about the known alternatives or outcomes or by estimating the probabilities associated to each. If a decision is reached by making assumptions about the known outcomes, three major decision criteria can be identified. The one chosen will depend on the decision maker's personality and on the magnitude of the consequence of error. The three decision criteria are:

Maximax, which assumes that the best possible decision will be made and therefore leads to the selection of the outcome that promises maximum gain. The decision is made to maximize the maximum gain.

Minimax, which assumes that the worst possible decision will be made and therefore leads to the selection of the outcome that promises the greatest minimum benefit. The decision is made to maximize the minimum gain if a gain is possible, or otherwise to minimize the maximum loss.

Minimax with regret, which assumes that the worst possible decision will be made, leading to a "regret" or opportunity loss. The decision is then made to minimize the maximum regret or opportunity loss.

Alternatively, the decision maker may prefer to estimate by "hunch" the likelihood of occurrence of each known outcome. This approach, known as the Bayesian approach, transforms the problem from one of uncertainty to one of risk.

Risk. Risk is the characteristic of events such that all their possible outcomes can be identified and such that each possible outcome can be assigned a probability of happening. Thus, risk situations can be assessed rationally in order to make effective decisions to guide actions. The main techniques of analysis for this purpose are described in the following subsections.

Probabilistic Analysis. When an event takes place, it may originate many outcomes. For example, the event "casting a die" may originate six different outcomes: the die has six different faces, each of which may come up. The probability of a given condition taking place is defined as the ratio between the number of favorable outcomes and the total number of possible outcomes. Thus, we can define the probability that X will happen as:

$$p(X) = \frac{\text{number of outcomes favorable to } X}{\text{total number of outcomes}}$$

For example, the probability that when casting a die, an even number will come up is 3/6, or 1/2, or .5, because out of six possible outcomes (1, 2, 3, 4, 5, and 6), there are three outcomes that are favorable (2, 4, and 6).

Thus, an outcome that is impossible has a probability of 0; one that is certain, a probability of 1; and any other conditions will be characterized by outcomes whose probabilities are between 0 and 1. A set of outcomes containing all possible outcomes of an event is known as a set of collectively exhaustive outcomes. In such a set, one of the events will occur with certainty.

When several outcomes cannot occur simultaneously, they are defined as mutually exclusive outcomes. For example, if a die is cast, the outcomes 2 and 6 are mutually exclusive: only one of them can take place at one time. When the occurrence of an outcome does not affect the probability of another outcome, then they are known as independent outcomes. Given two outcomes, the probability that one will occur after the other one has occurred is known as a *conditional probability*.

In many practical situations, the probability of a given outcome cannot be readily calculated. In those cases, it may be possible to estimate it from experimental observations. This is done by recording for a large number of events the number of times when the outcome sought appeared and considering its relative frequency (the ratio between favorable and total outcomes) as an estimate of its probability. For example, if we cast a die 100 times, and the outcome 5 comes up 18 times, we can estimate its probability as 18/100, or .18. The probability calculated by recording the frequency with which the outcome 5 took place is known as the empirical objective probability. The probability calculated by an exhaustive evaluation of all possible outcomes is known as the a priori objective probability. In the case of a die, the a priori probability of a 5 would be 1/6, or .16667.

A basic theorem of probabilistic analysis states that "as the number of events tends to infinity, the empirical probability tends to the a priori probability." In other words, as the number of times an event occurs increases, the frequency with which a given outcome will come up gets closer to its theoretical, a priori probability.

Describing a risk situation through objective probabilities is always desirable, especially if the a priori probabilities can be calculated. However, in real life it is often very difficult to enumerate exhaustively all possible outcomes of an event and calculate their a priori probabilities. Furthermore, it may be impractical to try to collect the necessary information to estimate an empirical probability. When such circumstances prevail, an alternative is to use *subjective* or *Bayesian* probabilities instead.

Bayesian probabilities are an expression of the decision maker's subjective estimate of the likelihood that a given outcome may take place. This estimate may be based on some historical data modified to account for the decision maker's perception of how that type of event may change in the future, or they may be based simply on "hunch." Thus, the Bayesian approach is especially useful to deal with one-of-a-kind events and also to transform a problem characterized by uncertainty into one of subjective but explicit risk evaluation.

Let us now review some of the basic rules for handling probabilistic outcomes. To this effect, we will use the notation $p(X)$ to denote the probability that outcome X will take place.

RULE 1: The sum of the probabilities of mutually exclusive, exhaustive outcomes is 1. If A and B are two such outcomes, then

$$p(A) + p(B) = 1$$

An important consequence of this rule is that given the probability of A, then the probability of A *not* happening (also known as the probability of not A) is:

$$p(\text{not } A) = 1 - p(A)$$

RULE 2: The probability that one outcome *or* another mutually exclusive outcome will happen is

$$p(A \text{ or } B) = p(A) + p(B)$$

RULE 3: The probability that one outcome *or* another *not* mutually exclusive outcome will happen is

$$p(A \text{ or } B) = p(A) + p(B) - p(A \text{ and } B)$$

RULE 4: The probability of an outcome A can be expressed as

$$p(A) = p(A \text{ and } B) + p(A \text{ and not } B)$$

RULE 5: The probability that two (or more) independent outcomes will occur is called their *joint probability* and is

$$p(A \text{ and } B) = p(A) \times p(B)$$

RULE 6: The conditional probability that outcome A will take place after a dependent outcome B has taken place is

$$p(A/B) = \frac{p(A \text{ and } B)}{p(B)}$$

RULE 7: The joint probability of two dependent outcomes is

$$p(A \text{ and } B) = p(A/B) \times p(B)$$

or conversely

$$p(A \text{ and } B) = p(B/A) \times p(A)$$

RULE 8:   As a consequence of Rule 7, we can derive

$$p(B/A) = p(A/B) \times \frac{p(B)}{p(A)}$$

This is known as Bayes's Rule.

RULE 9:   If each outcome of an event has a benefit as well as a probability associated to it, then the mathematical expectation, or expected value of the event, is the weighted average of the benefits, in which the probabilities are used as weights. Thus, if an event X has two possible outcomes, A and B, with probabilities $p(A)$ and $p(B)$ and benefits $b(A)$ and $b(B)$, respectively, the expected value $E(X)$ of the event is

$$E(X) = p(A)b(A) + p(B)b(B)$$

Decision Analysis.   At this point, let us examine a simple decision-making example to illustrate the application of the definitions and rules just developed and define some further concepts. The problem we will discuss concerns inventory management with risk. A newspaper stand operator must decide each day how many newspapers to stock; he or she can buy each newspaper for $.25 and either sell it for $.35, making a profit of $.10, or return it for a $.05 refund, for a loss of $.20. The fixed cost allocation to the newspaper is $5.00.

To solve this problem, we look at the demand for newspapers each day for the preceding year, and we find that it varied between 60 and 80 copies demanded per day (demand equals sales plus lost sales). The statistics are summarized in Table 5. There we see that, for example, between 60 and 64 newspapers were demanded 85 days of the year. In order to simplify the analysis, we will deal exclusively with the midpoint of each range, which is shown as the average demand. Thus, we say that 85 days of the year the demand was 62 newspapers. Since 85 days is .233 of 365 days, the probability that a demand of 62 newspapers will take place is then .233, and similarly for the other demand levels.

In this problem, we have an *event*: the daily sales of newspapers. We have four exhaustive *outcomes* of this event: demands of 62, 67, 72, and 77 news-

Table 5. *Example of Inventory Management with Risk: Demand Characteristics*

Demand levels	Average demand	Number of days for demand level	Probability of demand
60–64	62	85	.233
65–69	67	112	.307
70–74	72	104	.285
75–80	77	64	.175
	Total	365	1.000

papers. And we have, therefore, four *alternatives*: we can stock either 62, 67, 72, or 77 newspapers in a given day. The problem is to make a decision, to select the best alternative, given the event and its outcomes, and their associated probabilities. To this effect, we can build what is called a conditional payoff matrix, shown in Table 6.

The conditional payoff matrix shows the benefit, or *payoff*, associated with each alternative, for each outcome. It is called conditional because each value is valid under the condition that its corresponding outcome takes place.

In Tables 5, 6, and 7 we see, for example, that if the strategy followed is to stock 72 newspapers in a given day, and demand that day is 62 newspapers, the payoff will be:

62 newspapers sold at a $.10 profit each	$6.20
10 newspapers returned at a $.20 loss each	2.00
Gross profit	$4.20
Fixed cost allocation	5.00
Net profit (payoff)	−$ .80

Table 6. *Example of Inventory Management with Risk: Conditional Payoff Matrix*

Demand (outcomes)	Stock level (alternatives)			
	62	67	72	77
62	1.20	.20	−.80	−1.80
67	1.20	1.70	.70	−.30
72	1.20	1.70	2.20	1.20
77	1.20	1.70	2.20	2.70

Table 7. *Example of Inventory Management with Risk: Conditional Payoff Matrix under Certainty*

Demand	Probability	Payoff	EMV
62	.233	1.20	.28
67	.307	1.70	.52
72	.285	2.20	.63
77	.175	2.70	.47
Total	1.000		1.90

Similarly, we can calculate the rest of the values for the conditional payoff matrix.

Now we can calculate the expected monetary value (EMV) of each alternative, which is its expected value. Thus, we have for the first alternative:

$$EMV(62) = .233(1.20) + .307(1.20) + .285(1.20) + .175(1.20)$$
$$= \$1.20$$

In the same way, we can calculate the other three EMVs, and we obtain:

Alternative	EMV
Stock 62	1.20
Stock 67	1.35
Stock 72	1.04
Stock 77	.30

We see that the second alternative—stock 67—has the maximum expected monetary value: $1.35. Thus, given the information available, this alternative would be selected, leading to the action of stocking 67 newspapers every day.

However, the decision maker may wonder at this point whether additional information might be available, or could be developed, at a cost. Such information would enable him or her to increase the benefit by stocking different, more accurate levels on different days. This leads us to the question How much should we be prepared to pay to get additional information to increase our benefit?

In order to answer that question, we calculate the maximum benefit possible under the conditions of the problem. That is the benefit that would accrue if the decision maker had *perfect information*. Under those conditions, each day he or she would stock a number of newspapers exactly equal to the demand that would take place.

The results are displayed in Table 7, where we see, from Table 6, the maximum payoffs associated with each outcome. For example, if 72 newspapers are stocked and the demand is 72, the payoff is $2.20. Applying to those values the probabilities found in Table 5, we obtain the EMV for each outcome and the total EMV for the event: in this case, $1.90. This means that if the decision maker had perfect information, the total benefit would be $1.90, instead of the $1.35, which resulted from the strategy based on available information. Thus, the *expected value of perfect information* would be $.55(1.90 − 1.35). This is the maximum cost that would be justified in order to obtain perfect information.

Another important technique in decision analysis is that of decision making with revised probabilities. If a decision has been made on the basis of the information available, and a strategy—or coordinated sequence of actions— is being unfolded to implement the decision, additional knowledge about the outcomes will usually be gained. Under those conditions, the new knowledge may be used to reassess the probabilities assigned to each possible outcome before proceeding any further, and a revised strategy may emerge.

This kind of situation can be effectively handled using Bayes's Rule. We will illustrate this approach with a typical decision-making problem in resource administration. The problem concerns a marketing manager preparing to introduce a new product to a market: this is the event under consideration. The manager has identified two potential outcomes for the first year of sales: high sales and low sales.

Prior experience leads the manager to assign to each outcome the following probabilities—called "prior probabilities":

Outcome	Prior probability
High sales	.65
Low sales	.35

On that basis, he or she proceeds to implement the first action of the planned strategy: introduce the product in a test market and observe the results. The manager knows from prior experience that if the conditions in the market are favorable to high sales during the first year of full introduction, there is a high probability that the test will be favorable—he or she estimates it at .95. However, if market conditions are such that low sales will result during the first year of full introduction, there is a rather low probability that the market test will be favorable—he or she estimates it at .25. The latter two probabilities are conditional probabilities, because they express the probabilities for first-year sales that will result *after* the result of the test is known.

Given the manager's estimates of these probabilities, we can estimate the resulting probabilities—known as *posterior probabilities*—that sales will be high or low during the first year of full introduction. This can be done as follows: let us define H and L to represent high sales and low sales outcomes, respectively, and F and U to represent favorable and unfavorable test outcomes, respectively. If the marketing test is conducted, and its outcome is favorable, then we have:

$$p(H) \quad = .65$$
$$p(L) \quad = .35$$
$$p(F/H) = .95$$
$$p(F/L) = .25$$

To calculate the posterior probability of having high sales after we know that the market test was favorable, we apply Bayes's Rule:

$$p(H/F) = p(F/H) \times \frac{p(H)}{p(F)}$$

We know the values of $p(F/H)$ and $p(H)$; thus, we must first determine the value of $p(F)$. Using Rule 7, we have

$$p(H \text{ and } F/H) = p(F/H) \times p(H)$$

and also

$$p(L \text{ and } F/L) = p(F/L) \times p(L)$$

but on the basis of Rule 2, we have

$$p(F) = p(H \text{ and } F/H) + p(L \text{ and } F/L)$$

thus,

$$p(F) = p(F/H) \times p(H) + p(F/L) \times p(L)$$

and replacing the known values:

$$p(F) = .95 \times .65 + .25 \times .35$$
$$= .62 + .09$$
$$= .71$$

Now we can determine the posterior value of $p(H/F)$ from Bayes's Rule:

$$p(H/F) = .95 \times \frac{.65}{.71}$$

$$= .87$$

Therefore, on the basis of the additional information received from the favorable market test, we have a revised or posterior probability of high sales of .87, instead of the initial or prior probability of .65.

This and other decision-making problems can also be solved through the use of a technique known as decision tree.

Decision Tree. Decision tree is a technique of major importance in solving resource administration problems. As we will see later in this chapter, it provides an effective means of describing the characteristics of any decision-making process, such as those that characterize the life cycle of a resource.

To describe the technique, we will use the last example and draw a network, or tree, that shows all the elements of the problem. Such a tree is shown in Figure 28, where we use several conventions, as follows:

Nodes, which may be of three types:

Decisions, represented by diamonds, showing points in the decision-making process where decisions must be made.

Events, represented by circles, showing points in the decision-making process where events take place.

Terminals, represented by triangles, showing points in the decision-making process where the process ends, or where it is of no further interest to explore and describe the process. They are usually assigned a payoff value.

Links, also known as branches or forks. These can be of two types:

Actions, represented by solid lines, showing alternative actions that may be taken following a decision. They are usually assigned a cost.

Outcomes, represented by broken lines, showing alternative chance outcomes that may take place following an event. They are assigned a probability.

Going back to our problem in Figure 28, we can see that the decision-making process starts with an initial decision of whether to conduct a market test. If the decision is negative, we assume for simplicity that the process ends there. If the decision is to test, the action of testing follows, and an event takes place at the end of it: the results of the test are available. This event

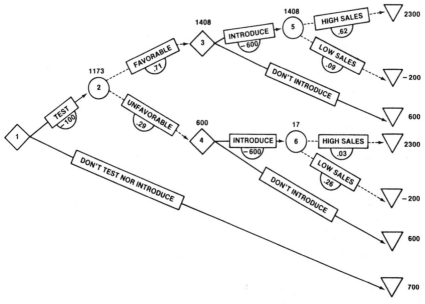

Figure 28. Decision Tree Example

may result in two possible outcomes: the test is favorable, which, as we saw, has a probability of .71; or the test is unfavorable, which therefore must have a probability of .29 (1 − .71).

Either outcome leads to a new decision: whether to introduce the product under those circumstances. If the product is not introduced, the decision leads to terminal conditions. If the product is introduced after a favorable test, this action leads to a new event: sales results become available. This event may result in two outcomes: high sales, with a probability of .62; or low sales, with a probability of .09. Both outcomes lead to terminal conditions.

If the product is introduced after an unfavorable test, this action leads to a new event: sales results become available. This event may result in two outcomes: high sales or low sales, both leading to terminal conditions. We can calculate the probabilities of the last two outcomes, as we did for the branch above, and we have:

$$p(H) = .65$$

$$p(L) = .35$$

$$p(U/H) = .05 \text{ or } (1 - .95)$$

$$p(U/L) = .75 \text{ or } (1 - .25)$$

Therefore

$$p(U) = p(U/H) \times p(H) + p(U/L) \times p(L)$$

$$= .05 \times .65 + .75 \times .35$$

$$= .03 + .26 = .29$$

Thus, following an unfavorable test, the probability of high sales is .03, and that of low sales, .26. We can see that the sum of all the probabilities of the outcomes leading to terminal conditions is 1.

The decision tree displays graphically all the alternatives worth exploring and their relationships. In addition, the technique can be used to guide the decision maker in the selection of the preferred strategy. This is done by adding to the tree information relative to the costs and benefits involved. For example, in our problem we could add the following information:

The cost of conducting the market test is $100,000.

The cost of fully introducing the product is $600,000.

High sales will be $3,000,000.

Low sales will be $500,000.

We have displayed the costs associated with each action, and the benefits associated with each terminal condition. The latter are determined by subtracting from the benefit expected all the costs involved in getting there. For example, if the manager tests and then introduces the product, and sales are high, he or she will obtain a benefit of $3,000,000 from which the manager must deduct $700,000 in costs, leaving a net benefit of $2,300,000. In the case where the decision is not to test or introduce the product, the net benefit is the $700,000 budgeted for those purposes, and thus saved.

With this information, we can now calculate the expected monetary value (EMV) of each alternative. This is done by working from the terminal nodes back to the initial node, as follows: We first calculate the expected value at each event node, following Rule 9.

Thus, for Event 5 we have, in thousands of dollars:

$$EMV(5) = 2,300 \times .62 - 200 \times .09$$

$$= 1408$$

and similarly for Event 6:

$$EMV(6) = 2,300 \times .03 - 200 \times .26$$

$$= 17$$

Now we can analyze Nodes 3 and 4.

In Node 3 we see that after a favorable test, introducing the product will lead to an EMV of $1,408,000, whereas not introducing it, to an EMV of $600,000. Thus we should introduce the product and assign the corresponding value of $1,408,000 to Node 3. In Node 4 we see that not introducing the product after an unfavorable test is preferable; thus, the value at Node 4 is $600,000.

We can now calculate the value at Node 2 in a similar fashion:

$$EMV(2) = 1408 \times .71 + 600 \times .29$$
$$= 1173$$

This value leads to the conclusion that it is better to test, than not to test and not introduce the product, which has an EMV of $700,000.

Preference Analysis. The problem just analyzed is, of course, a simplified representation of real-life situations. However, it contains the major elements involved in the decision-making process, except one: the decision maker's attitude toward risk taking.

Throughout our discussion on resource administration technology, we have used the EMV as a criterion for selecting alternatives. This may be a good idea when the amounts involved are not too large. When the amounts at stake in a risk situation are high, most decision makers will be reluctant to be guided by EMV, or play the odds, so to speak. Instead, they will look for an increasingly higher benefit than EMV, as the stakes increase.

Conversely, as the stakes decrease, decision makers will reach a point where they may take unusually high risks to try to obtain a larger payoff, because the consequences of a loss are decreasingly important. The former behavior characterizes a conservative investor, the latter a gambler.

The next question we need to examine is How do we account for the differences in attitude toward risk when arriving at a strategy? This is the subject of preference analysis. The tool of preference analysis is the preference curve which is a graphic representation of a decision maker's attitude toward risk taking for stakes within a given range.

The basis for constructing a preference curve is the concept of *certainty equivalent* of an event. The certainty equivalent of an event is the certain payoff that would leave the decision maker indifferent between accepting such payoff and taking the risks associated with the event's EMV. The difference between the EMV and the certainty equivalent is known as the *premium*. If the premium is positive, the investor is conservative, if it is negative, the investor is a gambler.

Given any event, we can then replace its EMV with the investor's certainty equivalent and proceed as before. This approach takes the investor's attitude toward risk into consideration. In practice, however, there are too many events with too many outcomes to consider. Thus, it is not practical to calculate at each node the certainty equivalent. Instead, a general relationship can be established, to be used at all nodes.

This is done, as shown in Figure 29, by plotting on the horizontal axis the maximum range of payoffs within which the decision maker must operate. The minimum payoff m is placed at the origin, and the maximum payoff M is placed at a point representing 1. On the vertical axis, we plot the decision maker's preferences.

If an event has a preference $p(X)$, this means that the decision maker is indifferent between getting a certain payoff X, or taking the risk $p(X)$ to gain M, and $1 - p(X)$ to gain m. The vertical scale, representing preferences, is set between 0 and 1; thus, it in a sense represents the probabilities associated with any outcomes. By asking the decision maker to express his or her certainty equivalents for different preferences—or probabilities—of M and m, we can derive a set of points along the preference curve.

To illustrate these concepts, let us consider an example, also plotted in Figure 29. If we have a range of payoffs between $m = 0$ and $M = 500$, we

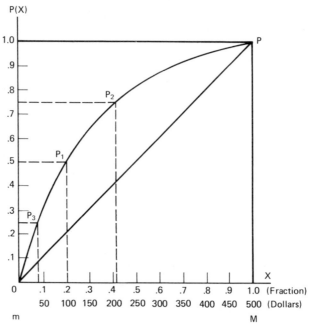

Figure 29. Preference Curve

can ask a decision maker to determine, by trial and error, the certainty equivalent of a .5 probability of 500 and a .5 probability of 0. If the answer is 100, we have point P_1. Since the EMV was 250, we see that the premium is 150: it is a conservative investor.

We then ask for the certainty equivalent of a .75 probability of 500 and .25 of 0, and we obtain an answer of 215, which is plotted as point P_2. Then we ask for the certainty equivalent between a .25 probability of 500 and a .75 of 0 and obtain an answer of 40, which is plotted as P_3.

The procedure can be continued until a few points are plotted. Then, a curve is fitted to the points, giving the preference curve for that decision maker within that payoff range. If the payoff range varies from small to large payoffs, the payoff curve may be an S-shaped curve, showing that when potential losses are small, the investor is a gambler, and as their magnitude increases, he or she becomes increasingly conservative. Such curves can be fitted using logistics curves or Gompertz curves.

If the curve has the shape shown in Figure 29, or a similar one, symmetric around $0P$, the equation

$$p(X) = \frac{(1 + A)X}{A + X}$$

can be used to fit the curve. The curve in Figure 29 has a typical shape. It was constructed with $A = 1/3$. The properties and fitting of this curve are discussed at length in Appendix A.

Finally, we can see that if the preference curve coincides with the line $0P$, the decision maker will decide on the basis of EMV.

Process Mapping. Up to this point, we have presented the main concepts behind resource administration. They center on two areas: the resource life cycle concept and resource administration technology. We now bring these concepts together in a map, or representation, that can be used as the basic specification for the development of an information system.

Information systems are the physical tools to implement in practice the technology for resource administration. To that end, let us first review the management process from an informational point of view, as illustrated in Figure 30. There we can see that the management process can be described in terms of the interaction between managers and the environment around them.

The effect of the environment on the management process is felt through events that take place, originating outcomes. Such outcomes are measured, or reflected, as data, which must be collected and compiled to form a data base. The data base makes data available to information systems, which

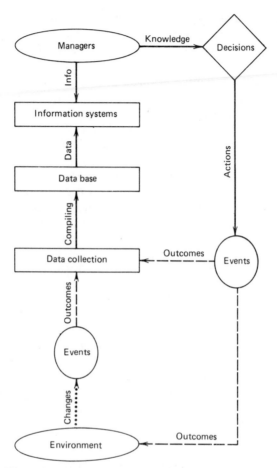

Figure 30. Informational View of the Management Process

process data, transforming it into information. Managers can then access the information provided by information systems and can also affect it through additions, deletions, and changes.

Managers integrate the information made available to them into their knowledge so they can state their problems, define alternative solutions, evaluate such alternatives, and arrive at decisions about how to proceed. Decisions are always followed by actions—doing nothing is also an action—which in turn affect the environment and also create additional data describing them. From this description, we can see that the management process can be described using the same entities that constitute a decision tree: events and their resulting outcomes, decisions and their resulting actions, and terminal conditions.

To describe fully the management process there is only one additional entity that must be introduced: *functions* that people must perform to ensure that decisions are made, actions taken, and outcomes handled. Functions can be defined at many levels of detail. For example, we may look at marketing, finance, production, and others as functions, or we may break those down into sales, promotion, accounting, scheduling, or go even further into sales planning, sales territory design, salesperson compensation, and so forth. The level at which functions are defined depends on the purpose of the definition: whether it is sought to describe an overall process in general terms, or analyze a particular process in detail.

The lowest level at which functions can be broken down in a meaningful way are *jobs*. Jobs are groups of activities that have common short-term objectives, close relationships with one another, and sufficient load to warrant assigning one or more people to perform such activities. The three characteristics we mentioned—objectives, relationships, and load—define jobs and their structure or organization.

Using the ideas discussed in this chapter, we can then map the details of the management processes involved in the life cycle of each resource. If we define a grid, such as that shown in Figure 31, assigning a column to each function involved in the life cycle of a resource, we can plot all the events,

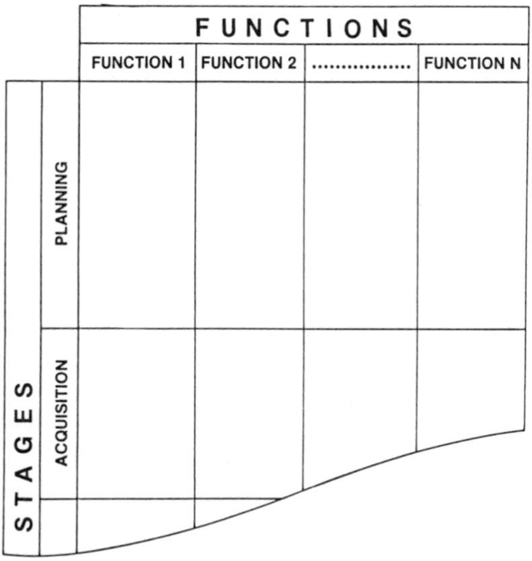

Figure 31. Resource Administration Process Flow Chart

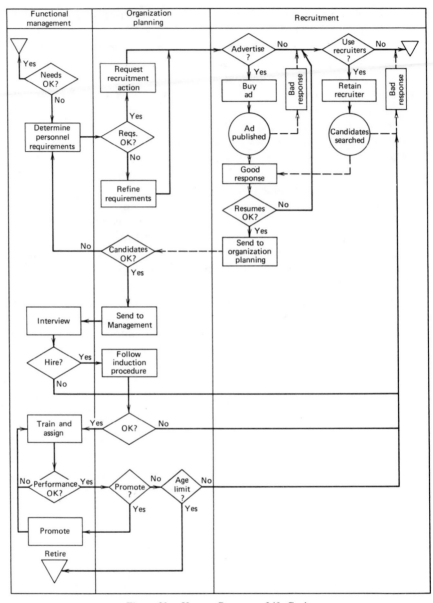

Figure 32. Human Resources Life Cycle

outcomes, decisions, actions, and terminal conditions involved in planning, acquisition, deployment, utilization, retirement, and control of that resource, showing which function is (or should be) responsible for every entity in the process. Thus, we obtain a decision tree, in which each node and link is placed in the column corresponding to the function responsible for its performance or handling.

To illustrate this technique, let us consider in Figure 32 a simplified, abridged version of a human resources life cycle. In it we show decisions as diamonds, events as circles, actions as rectangles preceded and followed by solid lines, outcomes as rectangles preceded and followed by broken lines, and terminal conditions as triangles. This technique facilitates the identification, analysis, and display of all aspects involved in every process during a resource's life cycle. The information contained in it is the first step in the definition of the information systems needed to support the management process in practice. The rest is outlined in Appendix C.

3.3. Resource Administration Efficiency

When resources are being administered, it is important to measure the extent to which they contribute to the system's output or performance. We will call such a measure the *efficiency* of the resource administration process. A simple definition of resource administration can be established by comparing the results obtained—such as profits—with the amounts of resources used in obtaining them.

Thus, if we define:

e = resource administration efficiency

O = system output

I = resource inputs

we have:

$$e = \frac{O}{I}$$

The value of e measures how well available resources have been used in meeting needs. From a different point of view, e measures how well the system is accomplishing what it is doing.

3

Resource
Management Systems

The essential characteristic defining resource management systems is that they are information systems. Informational resources integrate all resources in an organization. They are the resources that people use to manage physical and financial resources in a time-phased sequence. As previously defined, informational resources include data, knowledge, software, and hardware. Let us describe these in further detail.

1. INFORMATIONAL RESOURCES

The central informational resource is data. Data consist of symbolic representations of reality. For example, the length of a room, the cost of producing one ton of steel, and a musical note are each a data element.

A set of data assembled in a meaningful fashion becomes information. For example, the statement

$$\text{Total cost} = 2 + 3 \times \text{tonnage}$$

is a piece of information because it is a set of data—each element in the statement is a data element—assembled in a meaningful fashion. Such a statement is known as a model of reality. Thus, information is expressed in terms of models that relate data. Information that is organized in a meaningful context—that is, is classified and related—becomes knowledge when internalized by a human being. For example, a set of informational models defining all aspects of a steel-making process constitutes knowledge—or know-how—about steel production.

From the preceding outline, we can draw the analogy that data, information, and knowledge are related in an analogous fashion as raw materials that are transformed into components that are assembled into finished goods. The transformation of data into information is accomplished through processing operations, which may be automated. The assembly of information into knowledge is accomplished through thinking, which is currently hard to automate to a significant extent. Since data and its processed form, information, are the foundation of information systems, let us examine in further detail those two concepts.

1.1. Data

Data describe reality in terms of:

Entities, which are representations of all types of resources. They may represent **objects** or physical resources, such as facilities, equipment, or materials. They may be **agents**, or human resources, such as customers or employees. Or, they may be **transactions**, or financial resources, such as purchases, sales, or cash receipts.

Relationships, which are connectors that assemble multiple entities into a single, whole, more complex entity that constitutes a system.

Attributes, which express characteristics of entities and relationships. Attributes have values. Furthermore, they may be of four types:

Physical, such as dimensions, weight, time, and temperature.

Financial, such as purchasing or manufacturing costs, or interest rates.

Constraints, such as minimum and maximum capacity of a facility, or maximum capital available for investment. They are expressed numerically.

Conditions, such as statements of policy, or operating conditions. They are expressed in nonnumeric, logical terms.

Data can be of three types:

1. *Images*, such as graphs, pictures, or movies.
2. *Sounds*, such as voice or music.
3. *Characters*, such as alphabetic, numeric, or special symbols (period, comma, parenthesis, etc.).

Data can be physically represented by a wide variety of mechanical, magnetic, electric, or photonic (light-based) devices. In any device, data are represented either in analog or digital form.

Analog representation of data is accomplished by relating the value of an attribute to that of a physical magnitude, such as the intensity of an electric current. Digital representation of data is accomplished by expressing the value of an attribute through characters, such as letters, numbers, or special symbols.

Digital representation of data is by far the most important form and is becoming increasingly important in the representation of all types of data. In the case of images and sounds, the technology is emerging to represent them digitally instead of analogically. Thus, video images and sound recordings are likely to be represented in the future by digital means, expressing their major attributes numerically. For example, color hue and intensity or sound pitch and volume will be measured in arbitrary numerical scales, thus enabling their recording in the form of characters. This fact is of major importance because it presages the convergence of video, audio, and electronic data communications and processing technologies into a common format.

Digital representation of characters is currently accomplished principally by means of electromagnetic devices. In such devices, data characters are composed of impulses arrayed in matrix form, as illustrated in Figure 33. There we see a schematic representation of a magnetic tape (or other similar electromagnetic medium, such as disk). Along the tape we show six rows or channels, designated as 1, 2, 4, 8, A, and B, and the first five columns or spaces, which are numbered above the drawing. The intersection of each row with each column defines a position in the tape that can be either magnetized or not. In the drawing, we represent magnetized spots as black dots and nonmagnetized spots as white dots. Since each position (dot) can either be magnetized or not, it can be represented by a *binary digit*, that is, a digit that can be either 1 or 0. Thus, 1 may represent a magnetized spot, and 0 a nonmagnetized spot.

Each position representing a binary digit is known as a *bit*, which is an abbreviation of *binary digit*. A column of bits defines a character; these are commonly known as *bytes*. If we give values to each of the lower four rows, such as 1, 2, 4, and 8, and we reserve the upper two rows to provide additional combinations of bits, we can represent any numerical, alphabetic, or special character by a unique combination of magnetized bits along a column.

In Figure 33, the first column showing magnetized bits in positions 2 and 8 would represent the number 0, the second column the number 2, the third

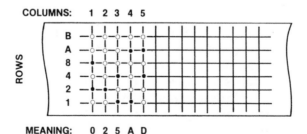

Figure 33. Electromagnetic Representation of Data

column the number 5, the fourth column the letter A, and the fifth column the letter D. By providing more channels or rows, we can expand the number of characters that can be represented in a given space or column. Most current standards use nine channels, of which eight are used to compose characters; the remaining one, known as the *parity bit* channel, is provided to enable a check of validity for each byte.

A data element, then, can be represented by a contiguous set of bytes, or *field*. For example, in Figure 33, the field of columns 2 and 3 represents the number 25. Thus, from an informational point of view, data are composed of nonrandom bytes representing letters, numbers, symbols, images, or sounds.

1.2. Information

We have seen that information is the basic unit or building block of knowledge. From an informational standpoint, information possesses several important characteristics, discussed in the following subsections.

Information Adds to Knowledge. Since a piece of information is the smallest increment of knowledge, any additional piece of information adds to the recipient's knowledge. In other words, information is "news." A corollary of this characteristic is that new (additional) information reduces uncertainty. Thus, from a physical point of view, information can be considered the opposite of entropy.

Information Must Be Communicated. In order to be useful, information must be communicated. Information residing in a file is not useful until it is retrieved and used. Information can be communicated verbally or by mechanical, electronic, electromagnetic, or photonic devices. In any case, it is transmitted as data to be assembled.

Transmission of data involves a number of entities, as described in Figure 34. The process starts with a sender or source, which emits a signal representing data. The data are encoded and fed to a transmission device, which feeds it to a communication channel that carries it to a receiving device. This feeds it to a decoder, which makes it available to the recipient, or sink, in an intelligible form.

A communication channel is always affected by two types of disturbances: noise, which is unpredictable and thus difficult to control, and distortion, which is the consequence of known causes and can be corrected or minimized. The characteristics of the transmitter, channel, and receiver determine the distance that can be reached by a communication system, which in turn

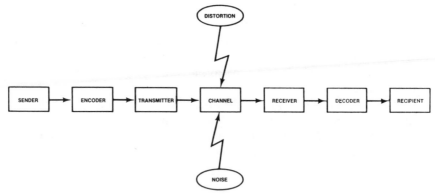

Figure 34. Entities Involved in Data Communication

determines the size and scope of human organizations that can use—or depend on—the communication system.

For example, the most primitive communication system is that of the human voice, where the sender encodes the message in the brain, using vocal cords to transmit and the air to carry the message to a receiver. Using his or her ears, the receiver receives the message and decodes it in his or her brain. Organizations based on this type of communication can exist only in small territories.

As the human voice is replaced by a tom-tom, or smoke signals, which can be carried farther, the size of the organization and its territory can increase and still be managed effectively, as an integrated organization. As communication begins to be transmitted by horse carriage, and then railroad, nationwide economic systems emerge. As those means are replaced by telegraph and, finally, satellites, a worldwide socioeconomic organization becomes feasible. At the firm level, the availability of worldwide instant communications enables the operation of global systems with increasing centralization of control.

Information Can Be Measured.   In 1948 Claude Shannon published his mathematical theory of communication, in which he defined information as the average number of bits that must be transmitted to identify a given message from the set of all possible messages to which it belongs. To illustrate the concept of information quantity (or content), let us consider a simple example. A sender and a recipient wish to communicate periodically and define for that purpose four different messages representing the possible conditions of interest to them. The messages are prenumbered in a given sequence from 1 to 4. We need to determine what is the minimum number of bits that could be transmitted to convey the right message.

Since a bit, by definition, can be in only one of two states (magnetized or nonmagnetized), which can be designated as 1 or 0, we can define the messages with different combinations of only two bits, as follows:

Message	Bit combination
1	00
2	01
3	10
4	11

From this, we conclude that the code size (in number of bits) or information content to transmit one of four equally likely messages is two. In general, if N is the number of equally likely messages that can be transmitted, the information content (I) is

$$I = \log_2 N$$

However, in data transmission not all messages—or characters—to be transmitted are equally likely. For example, in the English language, the most common letter is E, which appears .1031 of the time. In contrast, the letter J appears only .0008 of the time. Using one of the basic theorems of probability theory, we can adopt the frequency with which different characters appear as their probability of appearance. Thus, the average information that can be obtained is the sum of the products of each item's probability (p_i) times the logarithm in base 2 of the reciprocal of its probability:

$$I = \sum_1^n p_i \log_2 \frac{1}{p_i}$$

or

$$I = - \sum_1^n p_i \log_2 p_i$$

In our previous example, if the messages were not equally likely (their probabilities would not be .25 for each), but had the following characteristics:

Message	Probability (p_i)
1	.05
2	.20
3	.30
4	.45

then the information content would be:

$$I = -[.05(\log_2 .05) + .20(\log_2 .20) + .30(\log_2 .30) + .45(\log_2 .45)]$$
$$= -[.05(-4.32193) + .20(-2.32193) + .30(-1.73697) + .45(-1.152000)]$$
$$= 1.71998$$

Thus, we can see that when the probabilities of the messages are not equal, we need fewer bits to convey the message (1.71998 bits) than we do when their probabilities are equal (2 bits).

Information Needs Redundancy. To cope with the effects of noise and distortions in the communication channel, useful information must contain redundancy. Redundancy is the excess of information transmitted beyond the minimum needed to convey a message.

Using information theory concepts, we can define redundancy (R) as

$$R = 1 - \frac{I_u}{1}$$

where

$$I_u = \text{information capacity used}$$

$$I = \text{maximum information capacity of the code}$$

From the preceding discussion, we can see that data are structured at many different levels, in a fashion similar to that of the atomic structure of matter. The analogy can be displayed by comparing equivalent concepts as follows:

Structures

Informational	*Atomic*
Knowledge	Particle
Information	Molecule
Data	Atom
Byte	Nucleus
Bit	Proton

In this analogy, we see that a data element is the minimal description of an attribute pertaining to an entity or a relationship, just as an atom is the minimal amount of matter of an element. Similarly, a piece of information is the minimal amount of knowledge about a subject, just as a molecule is the minimal amount of matter of a composite substance.

Furthermore, in the same way in which we need to aggregate many molecules into large particles of matter in order to use a substance for practical, everyday purposes, we also need to aggregate information in a body of knowledge to expand its practical use. Similarly, we can continue the atomic analogy for such subatomic entities as the nucleus of the atom and one of its components, the proton, as the equivalents of bytes and bits, respectively.

1.3. Software

Software is the physical means to convert data, information, and knowledge into practical, usable information systems. *Software* is a generic term to designate programs or detailed algorithms to perform functions or execute procedures of calculations. There are three major types of software: operating, processing, and application.

Operating Software. This software contains instructions to steer a processing device (computer, robot, numerically controlled machine) to perform its intended functions. This is done by means of an operating system, which executes and controls all the individual operations needed to accept input data, process them, and make them available as output.

Processing Software. This software contains instructions to perform predefined functions on data within a processing device. These may be *utilities*, to sort or merge data files, for example. They may be *compilers*, to translate user-written programs in "high level," English-like languages to machine language, which can be used by the processor; examples are BASIC, PASCAL, COBOL, and FORTRAN compilers that translate programs in each of those languages to machine language. A program written in a high-level language is known as a *source* program. The program that results from processing a source program with a compiler to convert it into machine language is known as an *object* program.

An increasingly important type of processing software are data base management systems, which are software that can process data in a single "file" so as to make it available to a multitude of different programs and users.

Application Software. This software is the processing representation of knowledge; for example, programs to calculate a payroll or design a machine part are types of application software.

Operating and processing software are usually provided by equipment manufacturers or by specialized software design companies. Application software is typically designed and developed by the user, or acquired in the form of standard "packages."

1.4. Hardware

Hardware is the physical means or devices whose function is to gather, transmit, store, retrieve, process, and/or display data. The structure of informational hardware is depicted in Figure 35. There we see two major types

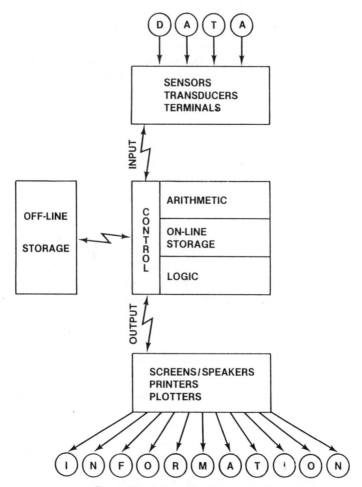

Figure 35.   Informational Hardware Structure

of devices: *peripherals* and a *central processing unit* (CPU). Peripherals may be:

Input devices, such as sensors, which measure physical magnitudes; transducers, which transform one type of energy into another type (for example, mechanical energy in a hydraulic flow into electrical energy that is used as a signal); and terminals, which are devices that accept data through keyboards, card readers, electronic pens, or voice, for example.

Communications devices, including encoders, transmitters, channels, receivers, and decoders to forward information to different parts of the processing hardware.

Off-line storage devices, which accept data, store it, and dispense it when required.

Output devices, including screens, speakers, printers, and plotters, which display information.

The central processing unit is the heart of the system. It performs four major functions:

Control, which is directed by an operating system that instructs the machine what to do with what data, when, and how.

Arithmetic, which performs all numeric operations on data—such as additions and multiplications—through the use of processing software.

Logic, which performs all logical operations on data—such as comparisons—through the use of processing software.

On-line storage, which stores all the operating and processing software, the application software being used at the time, and the data being processed at the time.

2. DEVELOPMENT OF AN INFORMATION SYSTEM

Informational resources are applied to the management process by means of information systems. Such systems integrate all informational resources and interface with the people involved in the management process.

2.1. Characteristics of Information Systems

Information systems may be manual or automated. Given the cost and performance of automated systems, manual systems are effective only when at least one of the two following conditions is important:

Creative thinking is of major importance. In problems involving unstructured thinking, such as the development of long-range strategies, or substantial artistic content, such as advertising design, automated information systems are of secondary importance because they depend on preestablished programs or thinking processes.

Unstructured data must be handled. In situations in which input data come in a wide variety of mediums and formats, such as handwritten, typed, verbal, and imaging, it is still easier to use manual procedures to "homogenize" the data before they are processed. A similar situation is the case of complex outputs that may require human intervention to explain.

Under most other circumstances, automated systems are bound to perform better, at a lower total cost (including penalties for errors). The main advantages of automated systems are that they can provide:

Network logic, which allows the solution of problems that require simultaneous computations of multiple process that affect one another. Human beings can think only linearly: from one topic to the next.

Large storage of information needed to solve problems. Human beings have limited recall capacity.

Large numbers of calculations without difficulty. Human beings have much more limited capacity to calculate.

High accuracy that derives from the total consistency with which machines follow instructions every time. Human beings are significantly more error prone.

Capability to execute complex algorithms. As long as the algorithm can be programmed, a machine can execute it. Human beings have significantly greater difficulty in learning and executing complex algorithms.

High speed. Machines can perform arithmetic and logic operations billions of times faster than human beings can.

Great flexibility. Machines can be reprogrammed easily. Human beings are more difficult to retrain.

Great endurance. Machines can work around the clock without interruption at a steady level of performance. Human beings cannot.

These reasons explain why automated information systems have been displacing manual systems in most of the world. Furthermore, failure to account for the significant differences between the information processing capabilities of humans and machines accounts for a significant part of the failures experienced with automated systems. When an automated system is developed that replicates a manual system, it is likely to fail because it does not utilize the advantages of automated machines. Rather, it performs human-like functions—usually clerical—containing techniques designed for linear logic and requiring a minimum of information search, speed, accuracy, and endurance.

From the point of view of their characteristics and scope, information systems can be classified in two types: *transaction processing* systems, such as accounting systems; and *decision support* systems, such as resource allocation models. In every management system, there is a hierarchy in which transaction processing systems, which support the actions involved in execution processes, provide the foundations, and decision support systems, which support the decisions involved in stewardship processes, provide the main structure.

From the standpoint of processing data, transaction processing systems are essentially directed toward data gathering and compiling, whereas decision support systems are mainly oriented toward data utilization. Thus, the former supply the data needed to support the latter.

From the standpoint of financial objectives, transaction processing systems are oriented toward cost reduction or cost avoidance, through a direct trade-off between hardware and software costs against clerical costs. Decision support systems are oriented toward profit improvement by means of trade-offs between all economic factors relevant to a decision, such as costs and service levels.

From the standpoint of human skill enhancement, transaction processing systems are directed toward skill amplification, that is, toward replicating human skills with greater speed, accuracy, and consistency in well-defined, repetitive situations. Decision support systems are directed toward skill transferring by acting as a mechanism that takes powerful yet complex techniques, developed by a few highly skilled people and applicable to uncertain, nonrepetitive situations, and makes them available in a simple fashion for effective use by many people with significantly lower skills.

From the standpoint of logic structure, transaction processing systems are characterized by linear or sequential logic; that is, every step of the logic flow is dependent only on the previous one. Decision support systems are characterized by network logic, in which a given step in the logic flow may depend on many other steps and may in turn affect them.

2.2. Human–Machine Interface Considerations

The interface between a system's hardware and its users is one of the most critical aspects of information system design. Even when an automated system has been designed to take advantage of the characteristics of automated machines, unless the input–output interface with the users is effective, the system will have operational problems. In this regard, human beings have important characteristics that must be considered. These are discussed in the following subsections.

Inability To Comprehend Large Amounts of Information. Human beings can focus only on limited amounts of information at one time. When the information presented is of different types—quantitative, qualitative, and judgmental, for example—the amount of information that can be understood by humans is further reduced.

Experiments have shown that given a varying level of stimuli (input), either physical or psychological, people react as shown in Figure 36. There we see that a stimulus must reach a minimum level (or threshold) before it elicits any response. For example, a person holding a weight will not notice an addition to it unless the additional weight exceeds a minimum value. Similarly, a person confronted with a certain amount of information will not notice—or be able to use—an additional amount of information, unless it exceeds a certain threshold.

On the other hand, when the stimulus exceeds a certain level, a phenomenon known as overload sets in, and response starts to diminish, as shown in the graph. Thus, from an information system design point of view, it is necessary to give significant attention to the amount of information displayed at one time to a user.

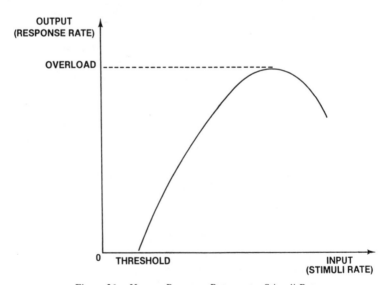

Figure 36. Human Response Rate versus Stimuli Rate

Limited Rationality. People's estimates of the likelihood (probability) of outcomes is biased by many factors, especially data availability and intensity of recall. Thus, if incomplete information is displayed, it might be used as if it were complete and could lead to incorrect decisions. Furthermore, recent events or events that left a vivid memory tend to be assigned higher probabilities of occurrence than objective observations would justify. Therefore, it is essential that a management system provide measures of data completeness and of historical frequencies of occurrences.

Handling of Data Detail. Experiments show that people make better decisions with summarized data than with detailed data. The reason is that they can more readily understand the whole situation. However, the same experiments show that when decisions are made with summarized data, the decision maker's confidence in its validity is lower than when the decision is made with detailed data. Therefore, in a well-designed information system, data should be summarized for decision making, and, in addition, detailed data should be provided as optional backup.

Limited Capacity for Simultaneous Communications. As the number of people that must be involved in a process increases, the number of possible communication links between them increases even faster. For example, if two people must communicate, there is one communication link between them; if three people must communicate, there will be three possible links between them. In general, if n people need to communicate, the number of potential communication links (l) between them will be:

$$l = \frac{n(n-1)}{2}$$

Thus, it is advisable to design systems that minimize the number of communication links needed to operate them. This can be accomplished through:

Modularization, that is, breaking the system into self-contained modules that relate among themselves.

Simplification, that is, elimination of all nonessential features and functions, limiting the number of people needed and the needs to communicate.

Decoupling, that is, the provision of features that enable different related functions of a system to operate in a quasi-autonomous way. Decoupling can be accomplished by providing buffers, such as information storage devices, or slack, such as excess capacity to process at different functions. *Standardization*, whereby certain conditions can be assumed, without need to communicate their status.

As a corollary of these observations, we can also conclude that as communications capability increases and its quality improves, the need for modularization, simplification, decoupling, and standardization decreases.

Need for Feedback.   Human beings behave in a goal-seeking fashion; that is, they set goals and then act so as to attain them. For this reason, people need feedback from any system they interact with to determine periodically whether they are approaching their goals and whether the system has received all their inputs.

Thus, an essential characteristic of an information system must be to feed back to the users the state of the system at frequent enough intervals. This is a more limited application of the feedback principle discussed in the context of resource administration. Nevertheless, the principle is the same, and its application is necessary for the same reason: to provide stability to the system.

2.3.   Major Technological Considerations

Although every aspect of management system technology is undergoing continuous, major changes, there are two types of technology that have emerged as the most effective means of developing, implementing, and using information systems. These are a data base orientation and distributed processing. Let us examine the main characteristics of these technologies.

Data Base.   The simplest way to explain the characteristics of a data base–oriented system is to compare it with the earlier, file-oriented systems. In a file-oriented system, as illustrated in Figure 37, each application program must be processed with the use of a set of files. A file is a collection of analogous records; a record is a set of related data items, or fields. For example, an inventory record may contain the following data items: part number, part description, part unit price, reorder quantity, reorder point, and safety stock. Each item in inventory would then be represented by one record, containing the values of each data field defined, in the format defined. The set of all inventory records would constitute an inventory file.

In the example in Figure 37, we see that Program 1 uses Files A, B, and C. Furthermore, we see that File A contains data items a, b, and c; File B

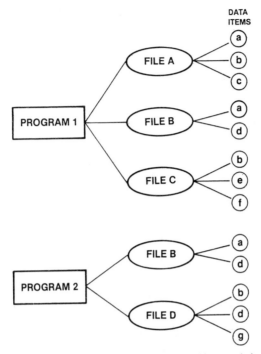

Figure 37. File-Oriented System Processing Characteristics

contains data items a and d; and File C contains data items b, e, and f. Similarly, we see that Program 2 uses Files B and D.

This type of data structure evolved because of the constraints in size and cost of earlier computers. However, as hardware size grew beyond practically constraining limits, and its unit cost decreased steadily, it became increasingly clear that file-oriented processing systems had many serious limitations that created barriers opposing their successful use and expansion beyond rather small limits. The main problems presented by file-oriented systems are:

Data is not versatile. Since different management functions tend to develop their own applications, they also develop their own data files. As a consequence, analogous data must be stored in multiple files but in different formats, different levels of detail, expressed at different levels of accuracy. Oftentimes, the equivalent data item may have different values in different files.

Data is duplicated. Data items are duplicated—knowingly or unknowingly—in many files. Thus, files contain much more data than really needed and are more difficult to keep up to date. As a consequence, such data can be used only in the programs that were originally designed around it. In addition, related decisions become incompatible because the data they are based on are incompatible.

Programs are inflexible. Since program logic is developed using such data characteristics as coding systems and breakdown levels, whenever data must be changed—expanded, deleted, broken down, or consolidated—either programs must be rewritten or masses of data must be recoded.

Under those conditions, it becomes exceedingly difficult to manage data in an efficient manner, capable of supporting all users and applications. The solution to those problems consists in structuring data in a data base environment, as illustrated in Figure 38. There we see that all programs access one single "file" or data pool containing every data item needed for all applications. This is done by storing data at the lowest level of detail needed and providing rules for its aggregation for different applications.

In addition, data base systems eliminate duplicated data items; however, they may contain redundant data by design in order to expedite processing. This makes it easier to maintain accurate, up-to-date data for all applications.

Furthermore, a data base structure makes it possible to develop programs that are data independent. Thus, if either data or programs change, it is not necessary to change the other. Another major advantage of data-independent programs is that it becomes much simpler and faster to reassemble data in new ways to provide special displays and reports. To gain all of the above mentioned advantages, a data base–oriented system must be structured around six basic elements, illustrated in Figure 39:

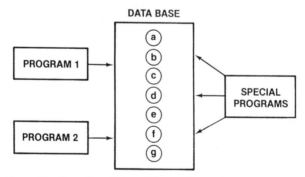

Figure 38.   Data Base–Oriented System Processing Characteristics

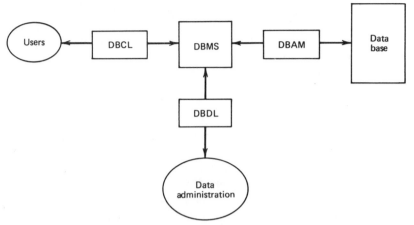

Figure 39. Data Base System Elements

1. *Data administration.* This is a special function needed to accomplish the following tasks:
   a. *Define data,* that is, establish the precise meaning of each data item in the data base in a data dictionary and define relationships among the different data items. The definitions of relationships among data enable users to assemble data in *schema,* or data sets that are needed for particular applications.
   b. *Ensure data security and integrity,* by controlling who should be responsible for updating each data item and who should have access to which data.
2. *Data base description language (DBDL),* which is used by data administrators to define the schemas needed in the data base.
3. *Data base management system (DBMS),* to execute, coordinate, and control the operations needed to access the data base by user programs.
4. *Data base (DB),* to store and dispense data off-line.
5. *Data base access method (DBAM),* which consists of a collection of programs or "routines" that access data or schemas in the data base.
6. *Data base command language (DBCL),* which enables the users to access the DBMS, to procure data and run programs.

Distributed Data Processing (DDP). The other major technological consideration in the development of management systems is the clear trend toward DDP and away from centralized data processing. The alternatives to deploy information hardware are illustrated in Figure 40. There we see in Figure 40*a* the sketch of a centralized system, in which there is a single central computer used by all users in the system, either by sending or transmitting jobs for processing.

In Figure 40*b* we see the sketch of a decentralized system, in which several independent computers serve different users. The computers may or may not be tied by communications links. Tie-ups are usually provided to exchange periodic information and for backup purposes. This type of system is disappearing and is being replaced by distributed data processing systems.

In Figure 40*c* we see the sketch of a distributed data processing system. Its main characteristic is that it is an integrated network of many linked computers. Each computer supports a group of users by performing either all their processing requirements or some of the processing in site and transferring the rest to higher-level computers—known as hosts—that perform the rest of the processing at one or more levels.

A DDP system essentially replicates electronically the organization structure, by making available at each function enough processing capability to support it. Its main difference with a decentralized system is that in DDP all processing is linked in one processing system. Typically, in a DDP system data are periodically summarized and transmitted to a higher level. The highest-level host contains, then, all the information needed to describe the functioning and state of the enterprise. It is the processing equivalent of the organization's head. The main characteristics of DDP are:

1. *Increased power at lower costs.* As processing technology progresses, smaller computers—miniprocessors and microprocessors—become increasingly powerful (can store, retrieve, and process increasing amounts of data faster) and at decreasing unit costs. Thus, "personal" computers linked to an organization's network become more practical to support each user.

2. *Increasing educational levels.* As more people acquire a better education that enables them to use more powerful quantitative tools in their work, the need for data processing increases. Furthermore, better educated people learn how to program and operate their own processors independently from a central group of specialists. This enables them to manage better under conditions of increasing uncertainty and complexity, since they can build their own models, relating many variables, to replace "seat-of-the-pants" management and can run them with short turnaround when conditions change.

3. *Access to archives.* The increasing availability of electronic archives providing data and information on a wide variety of subjects has

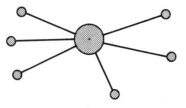

(a) Centralized system

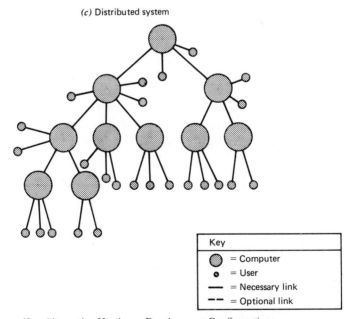

(b) Decentralized system

(c) Distributed system

Key

⬤ = Computer
◉ = User
—— = Necessary link
-- -- = Optional link

Figure 40. Alternative Hardware Development Configurations

127

increased the usefulness of small processors capable of accessing and using such data.

4. *Convergence of automated informational technologies.* The convergence of the technologies for data processing, text processing, process control, television, and communications has produced significant advances in the hardware and software needed to build networks of linked microprocessors in such a way that each processor can perform a variety of local functions and can also serve as a communication device to link local processes and data with the rest of the system.

Because of the increasing importance of DDP, it is useful to review its advantages and disadvantages by comparison with centralized systems.

The main advantages of DDP are:

Higher system-wide reliability for a given cost, resulting from the fact that when a local processor breaks down the rest of the system keeps working.

Lower start-up and communications costs.

Greater processing flexibility, resulting from better matching of processing power and needs, and greater ease of expansion and contraction.

Better and controlled turnaround.

More user involvement, with the consequent reduction in interfacing problems with data processing specialists and improvement in cost tradeoffs: users can better decide when to expand their hardware or their personnel or use outside services, for example.

The main disadvantages of DDP are:

More complex communications network technology is needed, with a consequent increase in system complexity.

The system is more dependent on individual user capabilities. As individuals change in the organization, the information system may change with them.

Other important considerations that are similar for centralized and distributed systems are:

Specialization.   In either environment, highly skilled specialists are made available centrally.

Standardization.   In both environments, it is recommended that all systems' development and implementation be coordinated centrally, in order to avoid incompatibilities and minimize unnecessary variety stemming from individual preferences.

2.4. Development Methodology

As discussed in previous sections, a management system should be the informational representation of an organization's mission, goals, and objectives. Therefore, mission, goals, and objectives define the point of departure of systems development.

We have also discussed the basic tool for analysis of management systems: the decision tree unfolded across functions. This technique permits the identification of the decisions that might be made, the events that might take place, with their possible outcomes, and the actions that must be taken to implement decisions and cope with outcomes. Furthermore, it identifies the functions that should participate to steer each resource through its life cycle.

We will now discuss how these concepts apply in practice in the development of management systems. The recommended methodology is described in the following subsections.

Describe the Current System. The systems development process should always start with a description and documentation of existing conditions. The reasons for this step are to achieve the following objectives:

1. Gain a thorough understanding of the system in operation, its main features, decision-making algorithms, event-handling approaches, data availability, and functions involved.

2. Identify problems that must be corrected and opportunities that may be exploited.

3. Identify existing features worth preserving or that must be preserved for legal or other reasons.

4. Quantify the workload that the system performs in terms of transactions to be processed and decisions to be made per day, month, and year, and the files that must be maintained, their size, content, and updating procedures.

5. Quantify the quality of service provided by the system, in terms of turnaround time, uptime, and the costs being incurred to operate and maintain the system.

6. Identify common decisions and actions (including reactions to event outcomes) taking place in life cycles of all resources, in order to bring out possibilities for unifying common policies, procedures, and, especially, data.

The description of the current system is based on the analysis of information usually collected by three means:

Interviews with a variety of personnel, ranging from top management to operating people. They are especially important in gaining insight into the perceptions of the people involved: how they think the system operates and should operate. Interviews are a good technique for obtaining information about the enterprise's stated mission, goals, and objectives, about perceived problems and opportunities, and about constraints that should be respected.

Observations of all phases in the life cycles of the resources involved. Direct observations not only should provide additional insight into the workings of the current system but also, and just as important, should be an opportunity to gauge how closely people's perceptions about the system correspond to the observed reality of it.

Compilations of data in tabular, graphic, flow chart, and other means, to provide measures of workloads, service performance, costs, and problems, for example.

Define Requirements for the Proposed System. The analysis of the existing system should point out the problems that must be solved and opportunities that can be exploited. These become requirements to be met by the proposed system. In addition, there are a number of environmental considerations that define further requirements to be met by the system. These include the need to meet competitive conditions and to comply with laws and regulations.

The requirements that management systems must meet to cope successfully with increasing uncertainty, increasing complexity, and persistent inflation were outlined in Chapter 1, Section 1.5, discussing the business consequences of exponential change. At this point in the management system development methodology, those requirements are introduced explicitly.

The purposes of this step are to establish:

1. What the system must accomplish to enable the life cycles of all resources to take place. This includes a complete definition of the decisions that should be supported and the types of transactions that should be processed to enable actions to take place.

2. How the system should reach its objectives. This step must identify each application to be included in the system. An application consists of one or more decisions to be supported or types of transactions to be processed. Furthermore, it must include for each application a definition of the data inputs and files needed, the algorithms to be used to process such data, and the outputs that the system must offer.

3. Who must be involved in providing what data, and using what information, for what purposes. Thus, in this step there should be a clearly established relationship between each application, the functions involved in providing data for it, and the functions using information from it.

4. The frequency and timing with which each input must be provided to the system to support all applications that use it, and with which each output must be provided to each function that uses it.

5. The volumes of data to be stored and processed and of information that must be displayed.

6. Specific hardware and software requirements that must be respected, including programming languages to be used and types of processing and communications equipment acceptable.

7. Financial constraints to be respected, such as amounts available to develop and operate the system.

8. Expected benefits to be realized from the system, including hard benefits, such as profit improvement, and soft benefits, such as intangible advantages.

To describe and document either the characteristics of an existing system or the requirements of a proposed system, there are many techniques available. These are discussed at length in specialized literature, such as the works mentioned in the Annotated Bibliography. However, to illustrate the major techniques available, we will briefly outline their main features here. The major techniques used to describe and document systems are:

Narratives in the forms of memos and reports. These are especially useful in documenting an enterprise's mission, goals, and objectives; the characteristics of hardware and software; knowledge available on different subjects; and data definitions.

Graphs, showing past, current, and projected values for major design variables. These typically include trends in data volumes processed per day and per month (average and maximum), service performance on a daily and weekly basis—including response time, processing time, and uptime—and cost trends.

Tabulations, containing backup data or displaying data characteristics, for example. Typically, data dictionaries are structured in tabular form, showing for each data item identified its source and users and its major characteristics, including measures of:

Relevancy, such as whether the data are timely, detailed, and useful.

Reliability, such as whether the data are complete, accurate, and precise enough.

Formats specifying the precise structure or layout of inputs, files, and outputs. In the case of outputs, they also serve to define their level of summarization and the sequences in which information is displayed.

Flow charts can be used to map resource life cycles, as shown in the example in Figure 32, and at increasing levels of detail, to define processing systems, algorithms, and computer program.

One of the most powerful techniques of analysis recently developed is known as entity–relationship (E-R) modeling. Originally proposed by Peter Chen, it has been used and extended by many others. Because of its importance, we will outline here some of its major characteristics as it relates to the methodology proposed. The entity-relationship technique analyzes and documents a process (or part of it) in five steps, described in the following subsections.

Define the Entities Involved.   As we saw in our discussion on data, entities can be of three types: objects, agents, or transactions. For example, if we wish to model the process of purchasing certain parts and paying for them, the entities involved would be "Purchases" and "Cash Disbursements."

Define the Relationships Involved.   Relationships establish links between the entities involved in the process. In our example, the relationship between purchases and cash disbursements could be "Payments."

Draw an E-R Diagram.   The data developed in the first two steps can be displayed graphically, as shown in Figure 41a. There we see entities represented by rectangles and relationships by diamonds and lines; the characters on the lines (n and m) denote that the diagram portrays multiple purchases and multiple cash disbursements.

Identify Relevant Attributes.   For each set of entities and relationships, their attributes relevant to the process at hand are then identified and their values stated. In our problem, the relevant attributes may be part number, purchase cost, inventorying cost, and purchasing quantity. For each entity in the "Purchase" set, their attributes will have a particular set of values.

This information can be displayed graphically in an entity–attribute–value diagram, as shown in Figure 41b. There we see that the values of the attributes enumerated above are: A-17, 17.50, 3.50, and 293.

Tabulate Data. After all relevant data have been identified and graphically displayed, they can be tabulated in entity–relationship tables, in order to facilitate analysis and documentation. To this effect, a data field that is common to all elements in the entity set and is unique enough to identify

E-R DIAGRAM

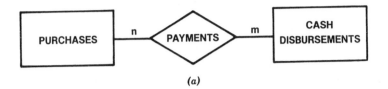

(a)

E-A-V DIAGRAM

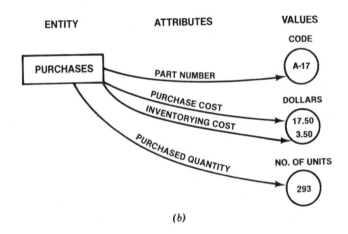

(b)

Attribute	Part number	Purchasing cost	Inventorying cost	Purchased quantity
Value set	Code	Dollars	Dollars	Units
Entity 1	A-17	17.50	3.50	293
Entity 2				
Entity 3				

(c)

Figure 41. Entity–Relationship Modeling Process

each element is selected as a "primary key." The table is then constructed in the sequence determined by the primary key. In our example, the E-R table is shown in Figure 41c.

The foregoing outline is of necessity condensed and slanted toward the concepts and techniques we have discussed before. However, it contains the main ideas behind the E-R modeling process. From it, we can see that this approach fits in well with the rest of the techniques discussed before for the analysis and development of resource management systems. This technique can be used effectively to detail the information developed with the use of decision trees to map the stages of resource life cycles. Furthermore, it can be advantageously used to design and document the details of existing and proposed systems.

Identify Alternatives. Once the requirements that the management system must meet have been established, the next step is to identify the alternative ways to meet them.

The first alternative to consider is *do nothing*. Under these conditions, it is important to develop a prognosis of what is likely to happen to the enterprise's performance. The prognosis is used as one basis for comparing other alternatives, as far as performance and cost.

The second alternative to consider is an *ideal solution* that can meet all requirements. That type of alternative usually requires the development from scratch of a completely new system and may be impractical for several reasons: because of the costs and risks involved, because of the time required, or because of the difficulties involved in "selling" and implementing it. However, it is worthwhile considering it for two reasons: first, because it provides another basis for comparing other alternatives; and second, because in the final analysis it may prove to be the best alternative.

After the field of alternatives has been bracketed within the two extremes represented by the first and second solutions, other alternatives should be defined. The additional alternatives should be defined, as much as possible, in terms of an incremental progression from the first to the second alternatives previously established. This approach greatly facilitates their subsequent evaluation. Each alternative should be defined in just enough detail to arrive at meaningful descriptions of its characteristics and provide acceptable estimates of the time, cost, and other resources needed, as well as the risks involved in its implementation.

The definition of each alternative should include not only details on how each process will be supported but also descriptions of the types and estimated quantities of resources that will be needed to develop and operate it. Furthermore, each alternative should include a general implementation schedule and an overall budget showing in gross terms the expected cash flows through full implementation.

Evaluate Alternatives. The evaluation of alternatives can proceed in many different ways. The technique proposed here has worked well in practice in a variety of project evaluation situations.

The main idea is to rank all alternatives according to their desirability and select the one that is most desirable. We can measure the level of desirability of an alternative by its *value*. This is defined as the ratio between the expected benefit to be accrued from and the cost to be incurred in the implementation of the alternative. Thus we have

$$\text{Value} = \frac{\text{benefit}}{\text{cost}}$$

Let us examine the components of that relationship. Benefits can be classified in two types: hard benefits, which can be measured in monetary terms, and soft benefits, which cannot.

Hard benefits can be obtained from three different sources, described in the following subsections.

Improvements in Cost Trade-Offs. These profit improvements accrue from trading off two or more cost—or revenue—elements in a system. For example, in a logistic system it may prove more profitable to ship by truck instead of railroad, at a higher cost, because the increased speed of delivery may allow a reduction in inventorying costs that more than compensates for the increase in transportation costs.

Improvements in Trade-offs between Performance and Costs. These profit improvements accrue from trading off performance quality against the costs needed to provide it. For example, in a marketing system, it may prove profitable to increase customer service quality and provide a lower incidence of back orders accompanied by a higher sales volume, while increasing the inventorying cost needed to provide the higher quality service by an amount lower than the revenue gain.

Improvements from Reverberation. These profit improvements accrue as an indirect consequence of actions taken to improve cost or performance trade-offs. Savings obtained by reverberation usually arise from certain benefits that were not explicitly considered in trade-off analysis. This may happen because such additional benefits may be difficult to estimate initially, or they may be simply acknowledged as additional reasons to reinforce a decision that can be justified without them. To illustrate this point, let us extend the previous example by pointing out that an increase in service producing higher sales may make it possible to reduce advertising expenditures. Although this effect may not have been included in the calculations leading to the decision to increase service, it may be measurable after the fact and included in the benefits tally.

Soft benefits may be obtained in two ways: from improved performance support and from intangible sources. Improved performance support gives specific benefits that can be indentified but cannot be easily quantified in isolation. Typical examples are the capability to perform sensitivity analysis on a solution to provide greater insight into its structure and the capability to retrieve information on-line, instead of through batch processing, to provide it faster and with flexible formats.

These examples illustrate situations in which benefits accrue from an automated decision support system by improving the quality or responsiveness of the information supplied for decision making, thus improving the quality of the decisions made using such information. However, in most instances, it would be difficult to calculate their monetary impact.

Intangible sources provide ancillary benefits expected to derive as a consequence of related actions but whose impact is generally hard to measure quantitatively. Examples of intangible benefits are the creation of goodwill or the reduction of noise in the working environment.

Costs can be classified in many ways. From the systems development point of view, it is convenient to classify them into five categories, described in the following subsections.

Development Cost. This category includes the costs incurred from the moment a system has been authorized and resources have been allocated to it until the system is ready to be implemented. Typically, the development cost is further broken down into categories such as business system design, computer system design, programming, software procurement, and system testing. Depending on the length of the development effort, these categories may be broken down even further. These costs are usually depreciated over the expected life of the project.

Implementation Cost. This category includes the costs incurred from the moment the system has been successfully tested until it is proven ready to run on its own. Typically, the implementation cost is further broken down into categories such as education and training, reorganization, data development, data coding, hardware procurement, dismantling, and salvage value income (negative cost). Depending on the length of the implementation effort, these categories may be broken down even further. These costs are usually depreciated over the expected life of the project.

Operating Cost. This category includes all the costs incurred from the moment the system starts running on its own until it is dismantled and replaced, except maintenance costs. Typically, the operating cost is further broken down into categories such as personnel, hardware, rent, materials, communications, and technical materials. These costs are normally broken down further to conform to the requirements of the enterprise's accounting system.

Maintenance Cost. This category includes all the costs incurred during the operation of the system to adapt it to new conditions and provide enhancements to the original design. Typically, maintenance costs are classified by type of service provided to the system. It is useful to separate maintenance costs from operating costs to facilitate subsequent audits.

Management Costs. This category includes all the costs incurred in planning, executing, and controlling all the activities needed to develop, implement, operate, and maintain the system. Typically the management cost is further broken down into categories such as project plan development, project plan updating, and project auditing. Depending on the duration of the system life cycle, these costs are kept separate for each of the stages identified above as major cost elements.

The categories used at each stage are normally broken down further, according to the organization's accounting rules and chart of accounts. Typically, for each category, detailed accounts are established for such cost items as personnel, facilities, equipment, material, cash, software, and outside support.

Benefits and costs, as defined above, must be calculated at yearly (or other) periods for the expected life of the alternative. This condition is necessary to provide an accurate representation of the cash flow associated with the alternative. This requirement, however, makes it necessary to introduce two additional parameters in the analysis: the *timing* of each cash flow, and its associated *risk*.

To account for the timing of the cash flows, it is necessary to discount them to a common point in time, such as the beginning of the project. That gives the present value (P) of each cash flow, which is expressed as

$$P = M(1 + i)^n$$

where

M = the amount of cash flow at its expected time

i = discount rate, expressed as a fraction of M per time period

n = number of time periods discounted

If discounting is done continuously instead of periodically, then

$$P = Me^{in}$$

Next, we need to introduce risk into the calculations. The risk associated with an alternative—or project—or with a particular benefit or cost in it can be measured by the probability (p) of achieving it. With this definition of risk, we can develop a relationship between risk and discount rate to be used. This can be done by defining a minimum or hurdle discount rate as the rate to be used when the probability of achievement is 1; that is, when the benefit or cost can be achieved with certainty.

We can then define a maximum acceptable risk—or minimum acceptable probability of achievement—for the variable considered, and we can establish the premium rate that would be demanded as compensation for the risk to be undertaken. Given these two sets of values, or points, other risk levels between the maximum acceptable risk and certainty can be interpolated by constructing a risk function, as shown in Figure 42. There we can see that when the probability of achievement is 1, we would use the hurdle rate h: that condition is represented by point P. When the probability of achievement falls to its minimum acceptable level R, we would use a discount rate r: that condition is represented by point Q. The discount rate r is the maximum rate, and the difference $r - h$ between it and the hurdle rate is the maximum premium.

We can construct a risk function by estimating the premiums to be paid above the hurdle rate for additional risk levels between R and 1, and then fitting a curve through the points obtained. Alternatively, we can assume a given function describing the risk function, such as the exponential function

$$i = Kp^c$$

and we can calculate K and c given the coordinates of points $P(l, h)$ and Q (R, r).

The exponential function works well in practical problems. Its use allows us to expand the discount formulas, to account for risk, as follows:

$$P = M(1 + Kp^c)^n$$

or

$$P = Me^{nKp^c}$$

Thus, using Bayesian probabilities we can describe simultaneously the effects of timing and risk on the cash flows associated to benefits and costs. Therefore, we can express the original definition of value as

$$V = \frac{\Sigma \,(\text{risk/time discounted benefits})}{\Sigma \,(\text{risk/time discounted costs})}$$

Using different assessments of risks, we can calculate the sensitivity of V to changes in perceived risk. That analysis allows us to identify the alternative with highest value within the risk range considered most likely.

Finally, the questions of including soft benefits and reverberation benefits in the analysis must be addressed. A practical method to introduce these factors into the analysis is to assign them arbitrary monetary values that reflect their relative importance in comparison with hard benefits. A similar

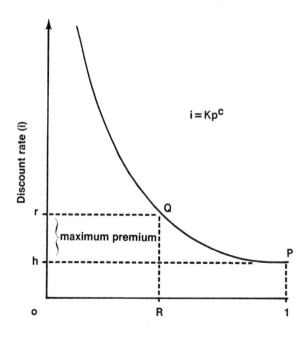

Figure 42. Risk Function

approach may be used to affect the monetary values for hard benefits, and sometimes even costs, by multiplying them by weights. This is done to introduce in the analysis intangible considerations and ensure that the values representing benefits and costs are as realistic as possible. When such a procedure is used, then the risk–time discounting technique is applied to the weighted values.

If alternatives have been defined as a progression from the simplest to the most complex, the value calculated for each can be used to evaluate the marginal contribution of each alternative. This evaluation is important because in many instances the values calculated for several alternatives may be similar. Under these conditions, the lowest risk alternative should normally be selected. If risks are similar, then the simplest alternative should normally be selected.

2.5. Specification of the Proposed System

After an alternative has been selected, it becomes the proposed system. At that point, one should establish additional specifications before proceeding to develop the system. Such specifications detailing further the characteristics of the system become a business system design (BSD). The BSD should include detailed definitions of:

Inputs: their sources, medium, formats, and frequencies.

Data base (or files):   its content, formats, relationships, medium, and updating procedures.

Outputs: their formats, frequency, and distribution.

Algorithms: including the formulas and procedures to be used to transform inputs and stored data into outputs.

Support systems: manual procedures, forms, and documents.

Coding systems: such as item, customer, and vendor codes.

Controls: establishing methods to verify data integrity throughout the processing system.

Security: including backup and recovery procedures.

Testing and acceptance procedures: for the final system.

Training requirements: for all users who will be affected.

Implementation plan and budget: containing details for the development and implementation phases.

The development of detailed specifications is the most critical part of the development process, because it sets the parameters within which the rest of the process must evolve. For this reason, at this stage it is important to ensure that the specifications encompass the major criteria for system effectiveness, including skill transferring, skill amplification, and adaptability.

Perhaps the most critical consideration is ensuring skill transferring. This is usually a problem because typically users understand the business but not the technology available to manage it best, and data processing personnel usually understand hardware and software, but not business issues. The most practical way to deal with that type of situation is to establish an intermediate group between the users and the technicians. Such a development group, combining both business and technical expertise in a consulting role, can act as a catalyst between the user and technical groups. The development group should be responsible for working with users to establish precise, realistic requirements; it should then translate them into a BSD. That document should be the basis for the development group to work with the data processing group in order to ensure that the technical design is acceptable.

The higher the skills available in the development group, the higher is the degree of skill transferring possible through an automated management information system. We can express that idea in the form of a *skill transferring ratio* (*T*), defined as

$$T = \frac{\text{developer skill level}}{\text{user skill level}}$$

2.6. Development of the Proposed System

The development of the proposed system should be the responsibility of the data processing group. Working from the BSD provided by the development group, the data processing group should develop the applications software in several stages. The typical stages are described in the following subsections.

Computer System Design. This design stage translates the specifications contained in the BSD into processing specifications, including:

Data base, or file structures and conversion procedures.

Hardware specifications.

Operational and processing software specifications.

Communications requirements.

Programming specifications, including system breakdown into modules that can be programmed separately.

Programming. The programming stage converts the processing specifications into applications software. In it, each system module is broken down further to define the smallest system increments that will become individual programs. Then, the logic to be followed by each program is flow charted in detail and checked to ensure that it reflects the system specifications and relates to other programs. Next, programs are coded following the flow charted logic and tested and debugged until they are shown to produce correct results. Finally, documentation must be produced to explain in detail the logic followed, naming conventions used and other details of each program.

Data Development.   In parallel with computer system design and programming, it is necessary to develop the additional data that new systems may require. This is usually done as late as possible, in order to minimize the need for updating it.

User Training.   Also in parallel with all the other stages, users must be given a complete program of education and training. Such a program should concentrate on the conceptual aspects of the system and on the uses of the information it will make available, in order to improve the quality of decision making and management.

Hardware and Software Procurement.   All the necessary hardware and software specified must be obtained, installed, and tested while the other stages progress.

Implementation Planning.   When the BSD is developed, it is necessary to establish a general implementation plan to identify the main sequence for systems development. Toward the end of the development stage, the implementation plan should be reviewed, detailed further, and assigned dates.

When all the stages outlined above are complete, the new system is ready for implementation. The success of the implementation phase will determine the success of the system. For this reason, it is important to review the basic ideas that should guide that process.

3.   IMPLEMENTATION GUIDELINES

Most of the technical problems related to management systems are found during their development and testing. However, the most critical phase in the introduction of new management systems comes during their implementation phase. The reason is that the simultaneous introduction of new concepts and new hardware to perform established functions, as well as new ones, always disrupts the culture prevailing in the organization.

Since disruption inevitably accompanies the introduction of new management technology, it is essential to take as many precautions as possible to make the implementation phase succeed. In this regard, there are a number of principles of proven practical value that are worth considering. They can be grouped in four categories: general guidelines and people-related, systems-related, and data-related principles.

3.1. General Guidelines

These guidelines apply to the implementation of any type of project. They are summarized in the following subsections.

Commit Top Management. The probability of success in the implementation of any project is directly related to the organizational level of its highest-level sponsor. For this reason, it is always advisable to ensure the open commitment of top management to back the implementation of a project. When top-level management is directly committed to the implementation of a project, its chances of success are highest. As the highest level of support for a project declines, its chances of success decline even faster.

Top management commitment means more than just approval. It means participation on a periodic basis to ensure that the objectives of the project are being attained and that their philosophy and intentions are being properly reflected.

Plan Ahead. Detailed project plans are essential to minimize surprises during implementation. Effective tools for project planning are network planning techniques, with which a project is broken down into subprojects, those into tasks, and tasks into individual activities. As a rule, activities should represent work increments that take less than one month to complete.

For each activity, there should be estimates of time and cost, as well as types of skills needed to complete them. Then, their sequence and precedence constraints can be established by structuring all activities in a network.

The discipline imposed by the need to develop a detailed plan usually brings to light many unsuspected problems and unanswered questions. Taking care of such situations in advance yields benefits that normally far exceed the cost and effort involved in planning.

Select the Correct Initial Application. When introducing a new type of technology it is important to demonstrate its benefits in a dramatic way.

This creates confidence and facilitates its further expansion in the organization. The right kind of initial application is one that meets at least the following criteria:

High visibility.   When the results become available they will be known by a good number of people who will be instrumental in expanding the use of such technology throughout the enterprise.

High improvement potential.   The results of the initial application should yield benefits important enough to encourage others to welcome its implementation in other areas.

Short time.   The initial application should focus on a situation that can be resolved quickly, in order to maintain the user's interest and attention focused on it.

Design from the Top Down and Implement from the Bottom Up.   The most effective way to design an information system is from the top down; that is, defining first the requirements of the highest-level user in the organization, and then progressively detailing the needs of the users at successively lower levels. This approach ensures that the system will have the correct focus and perspective and that as increasingly detailed data are provided at lower levels, they will be kept relevant.

On the other hand, the best way to implement an information system is from the bottom up; that is, starting at the lowest level in the organization, and progressively implementing applications for the higher levels. This approach ensures that data are collected at the lowest level of detail and are made available to higher levels as needed.

Do Not Underestimate Inertia.   Any system in operation possesses inertia, that is, resistance to changes in its status. Management systems are no exception. For this reason, when implementing new management technology it is necessary to cope with people's natural tendency to oppose change.

To minimize the impact of inertia, it is advisable to make every effort to make the users feel as integral parts of the project and to focus their attention on the benefits they can expect to derive from the new system.

Remember That Success Breeds Complacency.   One of the most difficult implementation situations is that of introducing a new system into an organization that is currently performing successfully. Although success may be obtained despite problems that keep accumulating and threatening the future, it is not unusual to find that a short-sighted attitude toward the need for new ideas is present in such organizations.

An effective way to cope with such circumstances is to place great emphasis in training and discussions about the importance of the new technology proposed. Unless that point is perceived, the organization's inertia will gravitate against the introduction of new ideas.

Depersonalize Conflict. The introduction of quantitative methods and automation technology usually results in solutions that not only are better than the ones obtained by empirical methods but also tend to be different in structure and characteristics. Their counterintuitive nature usually precipitates conflicts with users who are asked to look at old, familiar problems in radically new ways. This circumstance tends to exacerbate user resistance.

The best way to handle these situations is to adopt a common point of view with the users and agree to examine jointly whether the model is correct. This deflects resistance away from the people implementing the system and toward the system itself. As long as the system provides correct answers, the implementation team can work with the users to explain why such answers are better than the traditional ones, instead of defending a position.

3.2. Human Relations Guidelines

Successful implementation depends on fulfilling people's emotional and educational needs. For that reason, it is advisable to follow the steps described in the following subsections.

Ask Users What They Want. Users must always be convinced that they have been given every opportunity to express their viewpoints and needs in relation to new systems. Unless they have been listened to, they will not feel committed to the new systems.

However, it is incumbent upon systems designers and implementers to ensure that users get what they really need after they have had the chance to express their desires. This must be done in an open fashion, to avoid creating in the user's mind the impression that he or she is being outsmarted by the technicians. If this happens, the user will usually find ways to get even and thus defeat the best technical efforts.

Share Credit with Users. After a system has been proven successful, it is important to share the credit with users, even when they may have resisted the system's implementation. The reason is that in the long run only *their* system will work.

Invest in Training. The need to train users thoroughly before, during, and after implementation of a new system is as important as the technical details of system design. Without properly trained and motivated users, the best designed system will fail to perform according to expectations. User training should be performed in five different stages:

Preparatory, when the system development effort is starting. The purpose of this stage is to create among the users awareness that a new system is under development. The emphasis in this case should be on expected benefits, characteristics, and schedule of the proposed system.

Conceptual, as system development progresses. The purpose of this stage is to impart general knowledge about the application in question in order to expand the user's technical horizons in anticipation of the new system.

Operational, when the system is ready for implementation. The purpose of this stage is to familiarize users with the procedures and mechanics of data input and output, so that they are proficient in the operation of the system. This stage is essential to ensure a smooth person–machine interface.

Reinforcing, after an initial period of operation, to ensure that users are taking full advantage of the system's options and thus obtaining the projected benefits from it.

Auditing, to be conducted periodically to ensure that the system is performing according to specifications and that users are not resorting to "shadow systems" to resolve problems. Furthermore, audits are necessary to guide the system's maintenance and, at some point, its replacement.

Review Organizational Implications. A new management system will normally require some realignment of functions in order to perform according to specifications. These matters should receive thorough attention before and during implementation. Specifically, such questions as who should provide and maintain what data and who should receive what information should be clearly answered.

3.3. Treatment of Information Systems

The hallmark of modern, competent management is its understanding that information constitutes one of the critical major resources of any enterprise. This understanding is essential to guarantee the success of management information systems. In this regard, it is advisable to follow the guidelines described in the following subsections.

Invest in Systems. Management systems offer some of the best opportunities for investment in most enterprises. Thus, management should look at systems development, implementation, and use as investments necessary for a good return, and not as costs.

During the implementation of a new system, investment should include providing users with the necessary funds to try the new systems without affecting their contribution to profit. This approach facilitates enormously the users' readiness to give new technology a fair try.

Consider Operational and Political Needs. The development and implementation of any system cannot be guided by purely technical or even purely economical considerations. It is important to account for operational needs that must be properly satisfied, even when a direct reduction in cost may not be possible. For example, customer orders must be processed promptly and accurately, even when doing so may increase costs.

Furthermore, it may be necessary to assuage political needs in order to facilitate implementation and use. This may take the form of agreeing to design features that are dear to an important user, even when they may not be needed from a technical point of view.

Relate Systems to the Enterprise's Strategy. As we have discussed before, an effective management system is the physical representation of the enterprise's mission, goals, and objectives. Unless this relationship is direct and clear, a management system will become progressively irrelevant to the enterprise and will be limited to processing transactions.

Do Not Computerize Manual Systems. As previously discussed, automated and manual systems have substantially different characteristics. For that reason, and given the importance and economics of information systems, automated systems should be developed so as to maximize skill transferring and amplification and not to simulate clerical operations.

Design Systems for Future Technology. Informational technology can be expected to continue its fast-paced evolution for many more years. Under these circumstances, when a major new system development is undertaken, its design should account for the expected improvements in performance and cost that are likely to occur during its development and early use phases. In this regard, information systems design is a process akin to shooting at a moving target. Failure to account for such trends will result in investing money in systems that will be obsolete by the time they are ready for implementation.

Do Not Reinvent the Wheel.   A common problem with technical personnel is the tendency to look at the need for a major new system as an opportunity to display technical virtuosity rather than as an opportunity to improve managerial performance and return on investment. The usual consequence is the periodic reinvention of technology that is readily available.

This attitude results mainly from failure to account for opportunity costs. Full in-house development of a system, instead of selective acquisition of appropriate parts, results in appreciable delays in the obtaining of projected benefits. Thus, whatever new experience is gained in the process is gained at a severe penalty.

Design Systems Independently from the Organization Structure.   As pointed out in previous chapters, a management system should be designed around functions, not around jobs. Thus, even when an organization is restructured, management systems may continue to operate without change, so long as the mission, and therefore, the functions fulfilled by the enterprise do not change.

3.4.   Treatment of Data

As a corollary to the previous point, we can state that the better the data, the better the management. For this reason, in the implementation of new management information systems, it is advisable to follow the steps described in the succeeding subsections.

Invest in Data.   In our previous discussion, we have pointed out the dangers of using accounting-oriented data to support the decision-making process. Therefore, it is always advisable to invest money in developing and maintaining adequate data to support the enterprise's management process.

Provide Data Administration.   A typical symptom of a backward systems environment is lack of data administration. Under these conditions, data are developed on an *ad hoc* basis, and the management process takes place with whatever data happen to be available.

To ensure the preservation and enhancement of an enterprise's data resource, it is necessary to provide a high-level data administration function, responsible for developing and maintaining all the data needed to support the management process effectively. This function should include the responsibility for providing definitions, relationships, formats, and accuracy and precision standards. In addition, it should guard the safety of the organization's data.

Automate Data Development. One of the biggest obstacles to the implementation of new systems is the need to collect and maintain additional data. This job can be greatly facilitated by the introduction of automated means of data development and maintenance. This can be accomplished through automated coding systems, automated data gathering—done best when it is part of process control—and automated means to extract data from operational files, consolidate, format, and validate them.

Automate Information Display. The availability of high-level inquiry languages has made it possible for nontechnical personnel to interact directly with data files in order to extract and display selective data, as required. Such capability can significantly improve data availability in flexible formats, and, with it, the quality of decision making.

Use External Sources of Data. The increasing availability of automated archival services that sell data and information is of major importance in the implementation of new systems. These sources may enable users to set up their required data base in a minimum of time and with minimal effort.

4. IMPLEMENTATION OF RESOURCE ALLOCATION SYSTEMS

The most efficient way to state and solve a resource allocation problem is to describe the system under consideration as a network model, using the concepts we have previously discussed. In such a model, the nodes in the network represent *entities* involved in the problem; these represent fixed places, with resources whose levels are continuously varying. For example, nodes can be such entities as plants or warehouses containing material inventories that are being augmented through production or receipts and diminished through shipments; or, they can be cash holdings such as bank accounts that are being augmented through deposits and diminished through payments. Thus, nodes can be described as static inventories of variable levels.

The links in the network represent *relationships* involved in the problem; these represent movements of given resources between entities. For example, links can be such relationships as movments of materials, cash, or information between two nodes. Thus, links can be described as flowing inventories of constant levels.

Entities and relationships are characterized by attributes. In a resource allocation problem, these are costs, constraints, and conditions, as defined previously. Attributes are expressed by numerical values, such as purchase prices or financial limits, or by logical values, such as policy statements or contractual conditions.

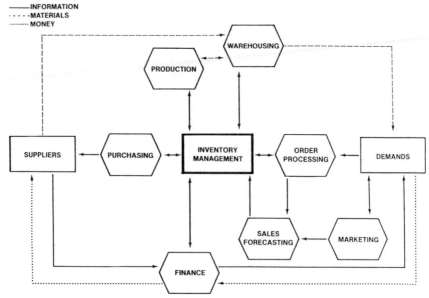

Figure 43. Major Operational Flows

To illustrate the practical application of these concepts, let us examine a typical resource allocation problem in a manufacturing company. The main operational flows are described in Figure 43, where we see the major flows of the physical, financial, and informational resources involved in some of a company's major functions and in its relations with suppliers and demands.

4.1. Basic Resource Allocation Questions

Looking at the company's structure and processes, we need to answer a series of questions that define the best allocation of resources. Such questions revolve around the need to optimize benefits. This may take the form of maximizing profits or return on investment or equity, or minimizing cost or unemployment, for example. Under those conditions, there are four types of questions that must be answered:

1. *Strategic* questions, including:
   a. What market segments should be served and to what extent?
   b. What prices should be charged at each market segment?
   c. What are the optimum levels of vertical, horizontal, and lateral integration? This defines the enterprise's external portfolio.

    d.   What is the total capital investment required?

    e.   What is the optimal capital structure, or equity-to-debt ratio?

    f.   What is the optimal investment structure, or fixed-to-liquid-assets ratio? This defines the enterprise's internal portfolio.

    g.   How many facilities of each type are needed and where?

    h.   What are the major characteristics of facilities? This includes their locations, missions, products handled, capacities, and costs.

    i.   In what sequence and when should facilities be added, expanded, or closed?

    j.   What are the delivered costs expected at each market segment?

2. *Tactical* questions, including:

    a.   What part of the sales forecast should be sold and where? This question is important when available capacity is insufficient to meet forecast demand.

    b.   What supply sources should be used and how?

    c.   What products should be produced, where, and in what quantities?

    d.   What products should be inventoried, where, and in what quantities?

    e.   What transportation arrangements will be needed to move materials into, through, and out of the company?

    f.   What is the expected cash flow for the period planned?

3. *Operational* questions, including:

    a.   Where should each customer order be produced and shipped from?

    b.   What supplies should be made available, where, and when?

    c.   What transportation rates and routes should be used to move what products?

    d.   What production plans are needed to provide the necessary inventories in the right places and at the right times?

4. *Analytical* questions, including:

    a.   What is the sensitivity of the optimal solution to changes in input values?

    b.   What are the penalties associated with nonoptimal solutions?

    c.   What is the cash flow breakdown associated with each solution?

These questions are of two types: problem-related questions, including strategic, tactical, and operational questions; and solution-related questions, or analytical questions.

Solution-related questions deal with the sensitivity of the solution to changes in input values or problem statement. Thus, they deal with the effects of uncertainty on the solution.

Problem-related questions deal with the optimal structure for the enterprise to fulfill its mission and meet its goals and objectives, as established through directional analysis. Such questions examine the enterprise's structure from the standpoints of its financial and physical resources structures. For example, the financial question of optimal level of integration is the equivalent of the physical resources question of the optimal production–logistic network structure for the enterprise. Thus, the financial and physical resources aspects of a resource allocation problem are modeled together, because the answers to questions about financial and physical resources structures are generally different aspects of the same problem. To facilitate the modeling task, it is usually practical to describe the problem in physical terms and include in the problem statement all relevant financial entities, relationships, and attributes.

4.2. Basic Concepts in Resource Allocation Modeling

To illustrate these points, let us consider the problems associated with strategic, tactical, and operational planning in a manufacturing company. In this regard, one of the most complex situations found in practice is that of the forest products industry; this complexity arises from the fact that all types of resources are of major importance in this industry.

We illustrate a typical material flow in a forest products company in Figure 44. There we see the complex interaction between land, facilities of many different types, equipment needed for production and logistic purposes, and materials flowing from suppliers, through the company's system, and out to demand markets. To answer all the questions stated previously, the material flow system can be translated into a network, as shown in Figure 45. There, each node represents an entity of interest, such as land parcels, suppliers, demands, and facilities. All permissible flows among those entities are represented by links, which define relationships between nodes.

Each entity and relationship can be characterized by attributes with values. These complete the definition of the model of the problem at hand. In our example, typical attributes provided by a modeling system would include the following options:

Nodes, which may have any of the following attributes:
   Costs, including discontinuous costs, such as fixed, changeover, and closing-down costs, as well as nonlinear continuous costs, representing operational costs with economies and/or diseconomies of scale. Costs are usually related in a tree structure, as discussed previously.

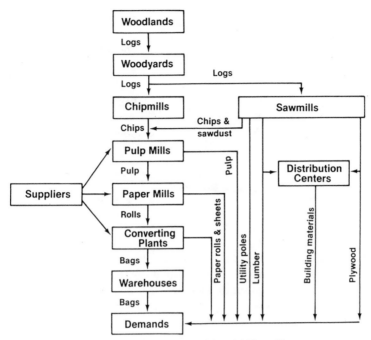

Figure 44. Forest Products Material Flow Chart

Constraints, such as throughput capacity limitations. These can be maximum or minimum constraints. Minimum constraints, in turn, can be conditional or unconditional. Conditional minimums are those that should be met only if the node should be in the solution; unconditional minimums must be met at any cost, and thus, they force a node in the solution having at least the prescribed minimum capacity. In addition, nodes may have other constraints, such as material balance equations, relating relative inbound quantities of raw materials and outbound quantities of finished goods, or product ratios, specifying that the quantities of products emanating from a node must be in certain ratios.

Links, which may have any of the following attributes:

Costs, including discontinuous as well as continuous costs, representing, for example, transportation, insurance, packaging, and other costs related to the origin–destination combination considered.

Constraints, such as minimum and maximum quantities allowed to flow between origin and destination for any product, or overall, or maximum time allowed for a flow to take place.

Subnets, or sets of nodes and links that are subsets of the total network. These may have any of the following attributes:

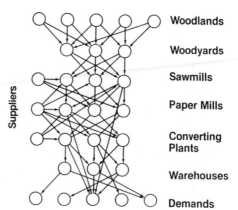

Woodlands

Woodyards

Sawmills

Paper Mills

Converting
Plants

Warehouses

Demands

Figure 45.   Resource Allocation Model: Network Representation

Constraints, or numerical restrictions, such as: "Given 10 potential new plant locations, we need a solution that has a minimum of 2 plants, and a maximum of 5 plants," or, "The sum of flows through one given set of arcs, or nodes, should be in the ratio 1:3.5 to the sum of flows through another set of arcs, or nodes."

Conditions, or logical, nonnumerical restrictions. These are represented by Boolean logical operators such as: *if-then, and, or, not*, and *nor*. For instance: "If product A is made in plant 1, then it should not be made in plant 2, or in plant 4," or, "All products delivered to demand area X must come from the same origin."

Once the nodes and links in the network have been established and their attributes defined, the result is an informational model of the problem at hand.

4.3. The Use of Optimization Techniques

A model can be used as a means of describing the essential features of the problem under consideration. That use alone makes it a valuable tool because of the completeness and precision it offers. In fact, the construction of a model alone provides enough discipline and understanding about the problem considered that most often it is enough to justify its development.

However, descriptive models represent only a fraction of the value that can be obtained from modeling and simulation. The greatest value of such techniques comes from the fact that a properly structured model can also be used to determine an optimal solution to the problem under consideration.

Many years ago, optimization models required large, expensive computers to run, limiting their value and applicability and forcing many users to settle for heuristic approaches to answer the types of questions discussed above.

The current performance and cost of computers has made it unnecessary to use heuristics in strategic, tactical, or operational resource allocation and planning. The cost-effectiveness of available data processing systems allows users to make extensive use of optimization techniques at low cost. From a managerial point of view, the use of optimization techniques in resource allocation problems eliminates two serious limitations of heuristics, namely:

It relies on an arbitrary selection of an approach.

It relies on past performance to evaluate the adequacy of an approach.

Arbitrary Selection. Since there are many ways heuristically to approach a problem, it is necessary to select one of the alternatives to deal with a given type of problem. This is usually done by trial and error, testing each approach with variations of the basic problem. The approach that yields most often the best solution is usually selected.

When properly done, the process of selecting a heuristic approach can be cumbersome and time-consuming, in order to ensure that the approach selected will work well under most practical circumstances. Furthermore, there are many instances in which the best heuristic approach will change as the input data change; thus, it becomes hard to select a general heuristic approach to deal with a general type of problem with consistent success.

Past Performance. Since there are no benchmarks to judge how good a heuristic solution is, the only criterion available for this purpose is to compare the heuristic solution to the past performance of the system under consideration. If the heuristic solution shows some improvement over past performance, it is adopted on the basis that it represents a step forward. If the heuristic solution does not show significant improvement, then other heuristic approaches may have to be tested. In either case, a heuristic solution is of limited use because resource allocation plans must deal with the future and must encompass the effects of external factors, such as competition and regulations.

By evaluating the adequacy of a heuristic approach on the basis of the system's own past performance alone, the impact of future developments and of external factors is disregarded. Since a heuristic solution cannot guarantee that the best possible solution has been found for a given set of inputs, the quality of a heuristic solution is generally of questionable value.

Thus, it is important to realize that in solving resource allocation problems, the power of optimizing techniques cannot be matched by heuristic alternatives. However, a word of caution is in order when using optimization techniques. The use of optimization techniques must be directed toward designing optimal systems, not just toward finding optimal solutions for given sets of inputs. This is the main reason for using the techniques of quasi-optimal analysis, which were previously discussed.

The use of large-scale optimization models based on mathematical programming techniques has proven to be a powerful, effective technique for resource allocation. Although most of its applications have been in problems requiring the allocation of financial and physical resources, they can just as well handle the allocation of human and informational resources. Thus, the technology currently available enables the allocation of all relevant resources involved in a problem, taken simultaneously.

One of the most significant recent developments that have made it practical to use large-scale optimization models is the development of generalized modeling systems, based on languages such as LOGS, that enable users automatically to generate large models, in minutes, instead of having to develop them manually over many months.

4.4.   The Modeling of Directional Analysis

Let us now examine how large-scale optimization models are used in practice to allocate resources in the contexts of strategic, tactical, and operational planning. At each one of those levels, the main objective is to integrate the main factors identified in the directional analysis phase—market growth rate, net price, product differentiation, and delivered cost—within the time horizon considered for each market segment. This is done by focusing on an objective function, whose value must be maximized or minimized. Typically, the objective function represents the total profit to be obtained, and since

$$\text{Profit} = \text{revenue} - \text{expenses}$$

let us see how the directional factors are accounted for in model inputs.

Revenue is determined by quantity sold and its corresponding net price. Quantity sold is input as a demand forecast for each market segment; this is in turn determined by market segment age and also by price, service, and product differentiation. Furthermore, net price is determined by availability (that is, the ratio between supply and demand), as well as by psychological and cost considerations. All these factors can be input in the form of demand curves by market segment.

Expenses can be expressed as the sum of operational costs plus differentiation costs. Operational costs include all costs related to procurement, production, distribution, selling, and financing. Differentiation costs include all costs related to product design and development, quality assurance, advertising and promotion, and service support. Thus, we can rewrite the previous equation as

$$\text{Profit} = \text{quantity} \times \text{price} - (\text{operational} + \text{differentiation}) \text{ costs}$$

And by assigning at each node and link of a network model the pertinent elements of demand quantity, price, operational costs, and differentiation costs, we can obtain an overall model summarizing all relevant characteristics of the problem. Then, using optimization techniques, we can find the levels of all activities represented in the model that maximize the value of the profit function.

Although profit maximization is normally the optimization objective adopted, other objectives or combinations thereof may be explored under different circumstances: for example, maximization of throughput or return on investment or equity; or minimization of cost, delays, or response time. In any case, it is always desirable to calculate the impact on profit of the solution selected and to compare different alternatives developed under different criteria.

4.5. Development of Strategic Plans

The allocation of resources is described from a strategic point of view in Figure 46. There we see that the alternative strategies are defined in terms of the mission, goals, and objectives to be contemplated. These are supplemented by forecasts of supply and demand conditions, prices, and costs and by restrictions to be observed, such as availability of capital or other resources. This type of information can then be assembled in a network type of model that when optimized yields the most profitable allocation of resources. That optimal solution is then the corporate strategy, which can be displayed in terms of a set of functional plans, such as procurement, production, marketing, or financial plans, or in terms of resource requirements plans, covering all major resources.

It is important to remark that in such an approach it is possible to reflect technical innovation and process productivity in the cost structures and the material balance equations used. Such factors are usually ignored in qualitative economic analysis.

When modeling strategic problems—usually covering a horizon of a decade or more—there are three types of approaches that can be used to formulate the problems. They are discussed in the following subsections.

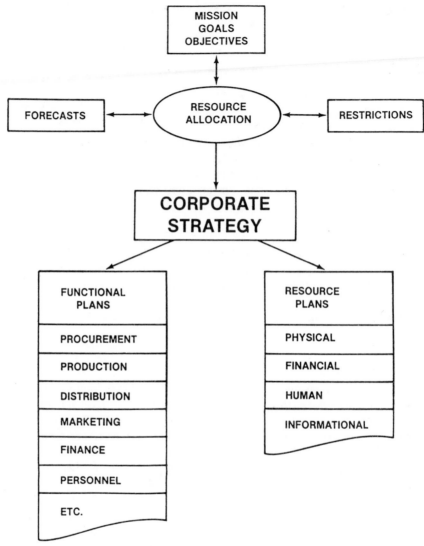

Figure 46. Strategic Planning

A Multi–Time Period Model.   In this case, data are developed to represent a number of successive periods in the future, and the objective function represents the total profit across time periods. This approach is generally preferred when policies or laws impose severe restrictions, such as the need to maintain employment levels or the need to maintain facilities in operation for long periods when expected inflation and long-term market growth rates are high.

Multiple Single–Time Period Models. In this case, data developed as above are used to find optimal solutions at different points in time from which an overall strategy can be evolved by interpolation. This approach is more efficient than that described in the preceding subsection from the standpoints of model formulation and analysis of results because it requires smaller models. It works well when the restrictions mentioned above are not great and long-term inflation and market growth rates are not too high.

A Representative Period Model. When long-term inflation and market growth rates are relatively low, it is easiest to model the problem in terms of a single representative period. This is accomplished by reducing all time series—such as costs, demands, etc.—to their financially equivalent uniform series throughout the horizon contemplated and then optimizing the system for the conditions reflected in the representative period.

4.6. Development of Tactical Plans

The allocation of resources are described from a tactical point of view in Figure 47. There we see that the basic inputs to such models are forecasts of supply and demand, costs, constraints, and conditions. Using the same modeling approach, we can calculate the optimal allocation of resources for the horizon considered, which becomes the tactical plan. As before, the solution can be displayed as a series of functional or resource-oriented plans.

Perhaps the most important tactical plan is the sales plan. It defines what products should be sold, in what quantities, where, and at what prices. Such quantities may be equal to or lower than the maximums stated in the demand forecast. The importance of the sales plan is that the accuracy of its execution has a major impact on the realization of projected profits. If sales personnel arbitrarily depart from the optimal levels established in the sales plan, profitability suffers: products sold above the planned quantities result in cancelled orders, and products sold below planned quantities result in excess inventories.

Therefore, we can see that a key to profitable tactics is to direct sales effort toward the fulfillment of the sales plan–neither more nor less. This can be attained by linking incentive compensation to deviations from plan: the closer actual performance is to plan, the higher the incentive compensation. In practice, some allowance must be made for cancellations, through some overbooking reflected in sales quotas. Nevertheless, we can summarize the

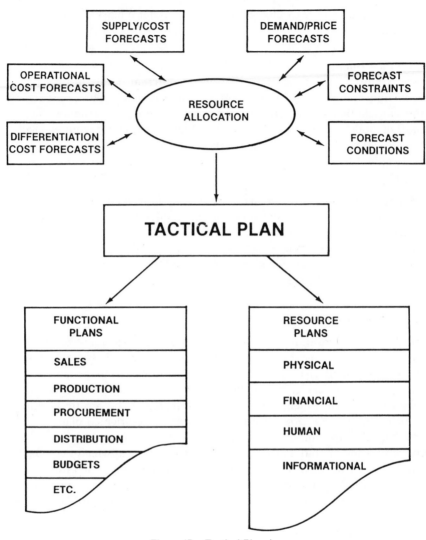

Figure 47. Tactical Planning

ideas outlined above by stating that the major element in a succcesful tactic is to follow the forecasting of the market with the marketing of the forecast.

4.7. Development of Operational Plans

The allocation of resources are described from an operational point of view in Figure 48. There we see that the basic inputs to such models are customer orders, expected operational and differentiation costs—usually standard costs—and planned constraints and conditions, such as machine availability and engineering production rules.

This information can be structured in a network type of model that can be used to allocate orders to production facilities so as to maximize profit. The solution from the resource allocation model can then be input to a production sequencing model that determines for each facility the optimum number, size, and sequence of product batches to be produced at each process. The optimal sequence for each facility can then be used to produce a physical resources plan, which may be detailed and displayed in terms of a procurement plan, a production schedule, and a distribution plan.

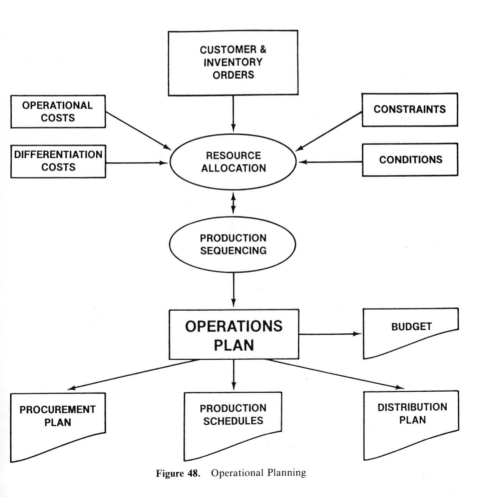

Figure 48. Operational Planning

4.8. The Use of Resource Allocation Models

To enable the practical use of resource allocation models, it is necessary to implement such models in the context of the enterprise's decision support systems. This is accomplished by providing automated data processing support capabilities that allow users to obtain the data needed to model a problem directly from data bases, with a minimum of manual effort.

As shown in Figure 49, the main functions involved in a complete resource allocation modeling system include the following modules:

Data extracting and formatting, which enables users to obtain and format the data needed to model a problem directly from a data base.

Data escalator, to transform automatically base period data into data representing any other period by applying growth factors.

Validation, to check all input data for obvious errors in format or in logic.

Model generation, to generate automatically an efficient model of the problem at hand. Model generators make use of high-level modeling languages that scan data in predetermined formats, deduce from it the characteristics of the problem, and generate the mathematical expressions needed to represent it. The LOGS language mentioned in the Annotated Bibliography was developed for such purposes.

Optimization, to calculate the optimal solution to the problem generated and provide the necessary functions to perform sensitivity analysis. These are general purpose mathematical programming systems that can efficiently handle a wide variety of optimization problems.

Report writer, to transform the data contained in the solution file from the optimizer in a series of reports meaningful to users.

On-line inquiry, to enable users to extract selective data on-line from the solution file. This capability is essential when dealing with large-scale models because it allows users to learn the characteristics of the optimal solution by examining it from different angles through displays or graphs.

The use of resource allocation models is described from a conceptual point of view in Figure 50. The key element is to promote the use of modeling techniques by operating management. Such users can be relied upon to maintain the data base needed to support the modeling system at the lowest level of detail and the highest level of accuracy needed. Their use of resource allocation models will normally be concentrated on partial, short-term models, providing operating guidance for the next few days or weeks.

The data contained in detailed operating models can then be consolidated automatically into higher-level, larger-scope models, which may use additional data from other files. Consolidation models are simply programs to

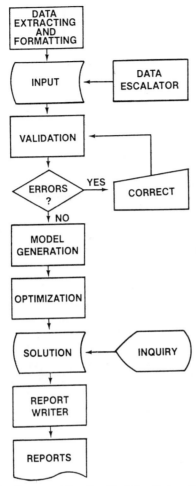

Figure 49. Resource Allocation Modeling System Components

scan available data, consolidate it, format it, and input it into a general resource allocation modeling system that can then automatically generate corporate models for tactical and strategic problems. Such models can then be accessed by top and middle management to obtain support in the decision-making process.

5. IMPLEMENTATION OF RESOURCE ADMINISTRATION SYSTEMS

The main purpose of resource administration systems is to support the decision-making processes that take place throughout resource life cycles. The

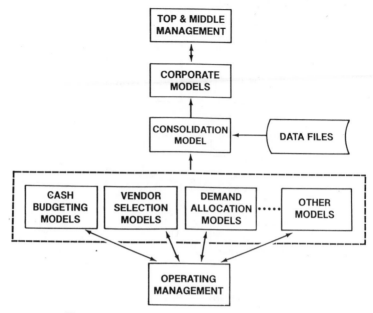

Figure 50. Resource Allocation Modeling System Use

problems encountered in resource administration are different from resource allocation problems in several respects. Perhaps the most important difference is that normally resource administration problems require fast responses and that therefore the timeliness of a decision may be more important than its degree of correctness.

Furthermore, all resource administration functions deal primarily with the workings of people, rather than with the allocation of resources. Thus, behavioral considerations are much more important in arriving at practical decisions leading to effective actions. For example, emotional and political considerations must consistently temper the results indicated by calculations. For the reasons stated, resource administration systems must make use of behavioral science principles as much as of automated data processing and operations research techniques. Thus, in resource administration processes it is impractical to assume full rationality on the part of people, and therefore allowance must be made to account for behavior that is nonrational from an economic point of view.

The main implication of these points is that in resource administration descriptive models leading to "satisficing" solutions may be more appropriate in some cases than are prescriptive models leading to optimizing solutions. Since the life cycles of all resources available to an enterprise are related, their resource administration systems must also be related. Furthermore, the use of a data base structure for such systems accentuates even further the need for closely coordinated design and maintenance.

From a practical point of view, however, it is simpler to design, implement, and describe the various components normally found in resource administration systems in terms of clearly delineated, particular systems. We will adopt that viewpoint to outline the main types of resource administration systems found in practice.

5.1. Physical Resource Management Systems

The most typical components of a physical resource management system found in practice are described in the following subsections.

Land Management Systems. These systems are of two types: record-keeping and mapping systems. Record-keeping systems are file maintenance and display systems used to store and retrieve data related to property characteristics—such as purchase price and mineral rights—or to site location characteristics—such as taxes, labor availability, and power availability.

Mapping systems electronically store graphic displays of property characteristics, such as maps showing property limits, buildings, and mineral deposits. These systems have proven extremely useful because they can store different types of information in different "layers" or drawings that can be combined and superimposed, as required, to produce different displays of property characteristics.

Facilities Management Systems. These systems center around operations scheduling and control and maintenance systems. Operations scheduling and control systems encompass production and logistic facilities and their associated equipment. Thus, we have production and warehousing scheduling and control systems, as well as process control systems linked to them, automatically to execute the schedules.

Maintenance systems, including preventive and corrective maintenance systems, are normally linked to scheduling systems, as well as to procurement systems and asset management systems. This ensures that preventive maintenance parts are available when needed and that correct decisions are made as to effecting major repairs or replacing facilities.

Equipment Management Systems. Since production and materials handling and storage equipment are managed as part of their facilities, equipment management systems deal primarily with transportation equipment.

The main types of systems used are operational systems and maintenance systems. Operational systems include fleet routing, scheduling, dispatching and control systems, rating systems, and stowage systems. Maintenance systems deal with preventive and corrective maintenance, as in the case of facilities.

Materials Management Systems. These systems revolve around inventory management applied to raw materials, components, work in process, finished goods, and energy. These include systems for procurement, record keeping, and inventory simplification.

Procurement systems support such functions as sourcing, purchasing, item acceptance, vendor control, buyer control, and coding systems support. Record-keeping systems deal with the accurate informational representation of physical inventories. Inventory simplification systems deal with item standardization and elimination of obsolete, redundant, and slow-moving items.

5.2. Financial Management Systems

Financial management systems have a dual role: on the one hand, they deal with the management of assets and liabilities; on the other hand, they provide general functions to the enterprise. The general functions they provide are based on the fact that all operations involve transactions such that at least some aspects of them can be expressed in monetary terms. Thus, financial systems provide the means to consolidate and compare all aspects of an enterprise's management through the use of a single common unit: money.

Financial systems, then, can be used to record transactions, measure exchanges, and to control and analyze the diverse aspects of resource allocation and administration. The main tools of financial management are the balance sheet, showing the financial structure of the enterprise—its sources and uses of resources—at a given point in time, and the profit and loss statement, showing the financial flows, or consequences, of the enterprise's operation during a given period of time. It can be said that in essence all financial management stems from analysis of the components of those two tools. The best way to illustrate this idea is through the use of the so-called DuPont Financial Model. Its structure is shown in Figure 51, where we see the main components of the profit and loss statement in the upper branch, leading to the calculation of the net profit margin, and the main components of the balance sheet in the lower branch, leading to the net asset turnover. Beyond these two branches, we see the definition of the two main measures of financial performance: return on assets and return on equity.

Although it is beyond the scope of this book to attempt any detailed discussion of some of the main techniques of financial analysis, it is impor-

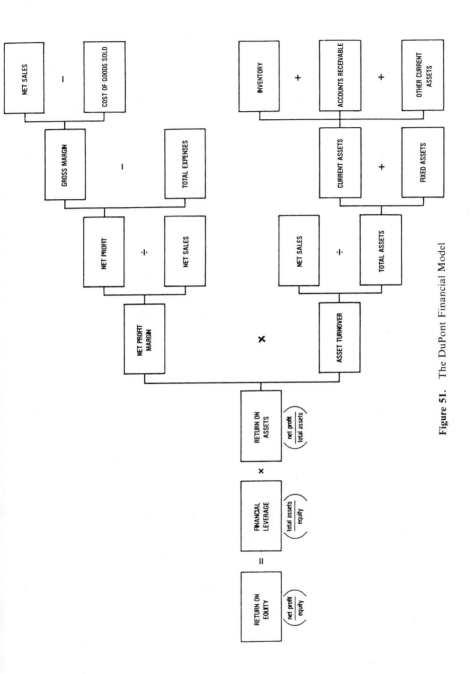

Figure 51. The DuPont Financial Model

tant to remark here that this is an area of management where quantitative techniques for resource allocation and administration have had great application and successes. The reason is simple: it is an area of management in which it is feasible to quantify most problem variables.

5.3. Human Resource Management Systems

Shifting the main focus of attention from functional to resource-oriented management requires many changes in perspective, as well as in definition. The most far reaching changes are required in the human resources area. The expression *human resources* has been in use for several years, but it has only represented a euphemism for the old *personnel* function.

Looking at the future from the perspective proposed here, we see that a major upgrading of the importance of human-related functions will become a critical ingredient in management success. This upgrading will take two forms: a substantial expansion of the scope of human resources management, and a significantly greater use of behavioral sciences throughout the management process. From such a perspective, we can project that the scope of human resources management systems should encompass all matters related to the activities and interactions among the protagonists who participate in economic life. Thus, we think of such systems as encompassing not only the traditional personnel management functions, such as recruitment, selection, placement, evaluation, and compensation, but also many other functions whose main component is the human element.

Among the functions that can be expected to gravitate toward the expanded human resources administration concept are promotion and advertising, sales management, market research, stockholders relations, public relations, competitive intelligence, and vendor control. The consolidation of all functions related by their basic focus on the human element should result in a synergistic relationship among those functions, which until now has been weak or nonexistent.

6. ORGANIZATIONAL CONSEQUENCES

This chapter has thus far outlined the major characteristics and directions of informational technology. Up to this point, we have concentrated our discussion on the technical aspects of development, implementation, and utilization of such technology. To put these matters in perspective, let us consider some additional information.

We have already seen in Figure 12 that the unit cost of information processing hardware has been declining exponentially and can be projected to continue to do so for several more years. Other projections made by independent sources indicate similar trends are taking place for memory capacity and processing speed: they are growing exponentially, while their costs continue to decrease exponentially. These developments indicate that between 1960 and 1980, the performance-to-cost ratio of information processing has been growing by a factor of approximately 100 every 10 years. Current research in this area points in the direction of similar growth rates through the mid-1990s.

At the same time, the number of computers installed in the United States has grown from about 5,500 in 1960 to over 700,000 in 1980. In the same period of time, the number of programmers in the United States grew from 30,000 to 275,000 approximately. Thus, between 1960 and 1980 the ratio of programmers to computers has declined from 5.5 to .39; current projections indicate that this ratio will be about .3 in 1985. The main reasons for this declining ratio are increasingly powerful operating systems that allow programmers to work more productively and increasingly simpler languages that allow users themselves to program many of their applications. This trend will strengthen with the increasing use of low-cost personal microprocessors linked in distributed networks. Such networks, electronically linking all persons in an organization, will significantly alter organization structures and their modes of operation.

The most significant organizational change that has begun to emerge in the last few years is the trend away from pyramidal organizations. These organizations can be described as tree structures. A tree is a special type of network in which every node is linked to only one preceding node. In such organizations, there are clearly defined hierarchical relations from top to bottom, each position (node) reports to one position above, and each position is assigned a specific set of responsibilities and authority levels, usually specified in a job description.

Tree structures were the most efficient way to organize large numbers of people when communications throughout the group required significant time delays, and when the amount of information available to the management process was limited and processing capabilities slow. Under those conditions, it made sense to modularize and standardize the work to be performed, in order to reduce the need for communications and processing. With the current and projected capabilities and costs to store, transmit, and process information, tree structures are clearly becoming ineffective in using such resources. Thus, they are being replaced by more flexible, network structures, which can take advantage of instant communications and large information storage and processing capabilities and which do not require modularization and standardization of work to perform effectively.

In a network structure, each node represents a person with a specific set of skills, education, and experience, not a position with a fixed job description. The organizational problem, then, is to integrate the people available into the enterprise in a way that takes maximum advantage of all skills available through the use of informational resources. The first step in this direction can be seen in the matrix type of organization that is emerging in the United States and Europe and in the even more general organization structures that characterize many Japanese companies. Some of the more important features of a network organization are described in the following subsections.

6.1. Task Descriptions

Since job descriptions are of little consequence in a network structure, work is described in terms of task descriptions, to be accomplished by teams of people bringing together the appropriate mix of skills to accomplish them. Under these conditions, a person may be a member of several teams accomplishing different tasks. Furthermore, a person's assignments to different teams will be changing in time as tasks are accomplished and the individual increases his or her skills.

6.2. Specialization

Instead of relying on modularization and standardization to cope with complexity, the network structure relies on specialization to establish operational links among the members of the organizaton. Specialization can be viewed in two directions: vertical and horizontal.

Vertical specialization occurs when the resource life cycle processes are performed. A first level of vertical specialization occurs in the structuring of stewardship and execution processes. Stewardship processes demand responsibilities, and therefore levels of skills, different from those of execution processes. Thus, in a network structure, the individuals concerned with planning and control can be conceived as occupying a stratum different from that of individuals concerned with acquisition, deployment, utilization, and retirement of resources.

Horizontal specialization occurs within a stratum in the organization's network and is a manifestation of division of labor, at a similar level of skills.

6.3. Multiple Reporting Relationships

In the operation of a network structure, every individual reports to several superiors at the same time. The most important reporting relationships for a person are of three types:

Technical relationships, whereby an individual has links to persons responsible for providing technical direction, education, and training.

Project relationships, whereby an individual has links to other individuals in each of the projects in which he or she participates.

Administrative relationships, whereby an individual has links to persons responsible for providing performance evaluations, salary administration, and fringe benefits and for establishing promotional adequacy.

In the United States, technical and administrative relationships tend to be concentrated, even in matrix organizations. In Japan, many companies split those responsibilities and assign them to different people. In both cases, however, network organizations focus on team responsibility and performance, rather than on personal responsibility and performance.

6.4. Electronic Proximity

The availability of electronically distributed information processing, whereby each individual has access to a terminal device, makes geographic proximity of little importance. Thus, many persons dispersed throughout the world can be brought together in a team to work on a task, with minimal face-to-face contact. This circumstance not only provides additional organizational flexibility in a network structure but also enables significant changes in the location of work. An increasing number of people can fulfill their duties while working at home or in any other environment they choose, instead of having to meet daily at a fixed place.

6.5. Resource Orientation

A network structure provides an ideal vehicle for organizing an enterprise along resource lines rather than along functional lines. In such an organization, each function is performed by teams of specialists in such a way that the teams' compositions and structures evolve continuously, as circumstances require.

A resource-oriented organization, as illustrated in Figure 52, focuses on the main resources of the enterprise. In such a scheme, specialists in the stewardship and execution processes of each resource type would be brought together to perform the necessary functions. Under those conditions, we would have:

Physical resources specialists, focusing on land and real estate management and on production and logistics functions involving materials, energy, facilities, and equipment.

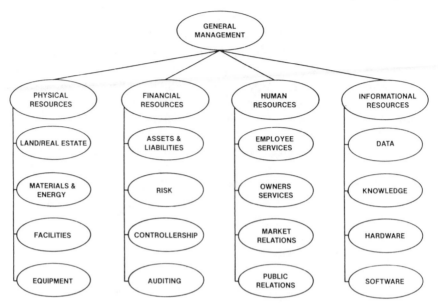

Figure 52.   Resource-Oriented Organization Structure

Financial resources specialists, focusing on managing assets and liabilities and risk and providing controlship and auditing functions.

Human resources specialists, focusing on employee services such as recruiting, education and training, performance evaluation, medical services, counseling, promotion, retirement, and compensation. In the same technical context, we would find specialists in owners services, such as performance reporting and inquiry handling, and in public relations, such as public communications and government relations. Furthermore, given the basic human content of relations with customers, prospects, and suppliers, we could find that a substantial part of sales, advertising, and promotion, as well as purchasing, would be integrated with other human resource management activities.

Information resources specialists, focusing on data administration and data base–oriented record keeping, as well as on hardware and software management. In this technical context, we would find generalized knowledge specialists performing such functions as research and development, engineering services, legal services, planning, and quality control.

A resource-oriented organization along the lines described above would be better suited than traditional organizations to cope with the shift from labor-based operations to knowledge-based operations.

On the other hand, such a type of organizational approach would present new problems. Not only does it require a shift from job to task approach and its concomitant shift from personal to team accountability, but it will also prompt important questions about who should have access to what information and who should control and protect what information. These problems must be resolved in each organization according to the specific circumstances. In any case they must be resolved in order to ensure that a resource-oriented organization network can function effectively. In this context, the most important action needed to ensure the success of a network organization is to upgrade people's skills through education and training and to enhance their capabilities through skill transferring. Continuous upgrading of people's skills and capabilities, together with improved information systems and improved data quality and accessibility, are the prerequisites of successful performance in a knowledge-based economic system.

4

Conclusions

As a consequence of the exponential changes in demographic, sociopolitical, economic, and technological factors in the world environment, the most pressing economic problem of our time is the need to improve productivity. This problem is especially acute in the United States, but it affects all nations in varying degrees. For this reason, it is essential to look at the characteristics and requirements of management in the years to come not only from a general resource management standpoint directed at trading off informational resources against all other resources. It is also useful to describe how such an approach can improve productivity.

Identifying the sources of productivity improvement is a good point of departure to analyze the best way to structure and perform management processes. Studies conducted by John Kendrick indicate that between 1929 and 1978 the main sources of productivity improvement in the United States have been technological innovation (or knowledge development and implementation), improved allocation of resources, changes in capital per worker, economies of scale, and changes in labor quality. These sources and their relative importance are shown in Figure 53. From these facts, we can conclude that the main challenge to managers in the coming years will be to find the means to ensure the most effective use of the human potential, the knowledge, and the informational technology available to them.

In order to fulfill an enterprise's mission and meet its goals and objectives, managers will find themselves integrating fast-changing informational and resource management technologies in the context of network-structured organizations. In practice, this will require a shift in managers' primary concerns away from the management functions needed to manage an enterprise and toward the management processes involved in the life cycles of the enterprise's resources. In that sense, we can describe resource management as an alternative approach to functional management: all the activities involved in the marketing, production, financial, personnel, R&D, administrative, etc., functions would continue to take place, but they would do so under a different structure and with a different perspective. With this in mind, we have outlined here how resource management and informational technologies can be used in practice to increase the knowledge content of economic

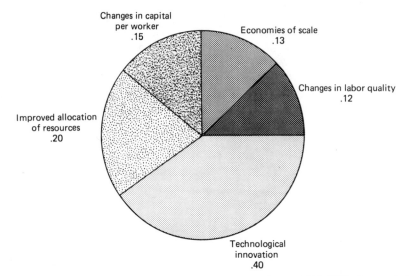

Figure 53. Sources of Productivity Growth in the United States (1929–1978). Source: John Kendrick (see Bibliography).

processes, to improve the allocation of resources and to determine the optimal levels of capital investment and the optimal size of productive processes, while also improving the utilization of an increasingly knowledgeable, better trained labor force.

The resource management technology we discussed above is the most effective approach currently available to ensure the best possible allocation and administration of resources. Its use in practice must be tempered, however, by the clear realization that economic factors alone do not fully describe the economic environment. We have come to realize that psychological factors—often difficult to measure—can play a role in economic processes even greater than that of economic factors.

At a macrolevel, we have seen in recent years that inflation is determined as much by psychological perceptions and changes in people's values as by the relationship between supply and demand. At a microlevel, it has been known for a long time that well-motivated people, with a clear sense of mission, are the single most important factor accounting for an enterprise's success. This point has been well documented in many independent studies. Some of the most recent research in this field, conducted by Harvey Leibenstein, confirms and extends that conclusion. As he expresses his findings, the key factor in productivity differences among firms and between countries is neither allocational efficiency nor any other measurable input in the productive process. It derives from management, motivation, and spirit—what he calls X-efficiency.

Thus, recognition of the importance of noneconomic factors is essential to ensure the effective, practical application of knowledge to the economic process. The application of knowledge to the economic process—fulfilled through the use of automated resource allocation and administration systems—is, in turn, the best hope we have to deal successfully with a future characterized by increasing uncertainty, increasing complexity, and persistent inflation.

Appendix A

Analysis by Contribution

1. INTRODUCTION

The idea behind analysis by contribution (ABC) is an elaboration of the findings of the Italian economist Vilfredo Pareto. Studying the distribution of income in different countries, Pareto found that a small fraction of the people always accounted for a large fraction of the total income in every country. Observations in many other fields have shown that Pareto's observations represented a general law describing the way in which the total value of a given parameter is distributed among the multiple elements of a set that accounts for that parameter. This concept has been known to work in many business situations and is usually stated as the 20/80 rule. For example, in any business it is generally found that about .20 of the customers represent about .80 of total sales, or that about .20 of the items carried in an inventory represent about .80 of the inventory investment.

The 20/80 rule is, of course, a rough description of the real situation. However, the basic principle underlying it seems to work in a wide variety of business situations, with different ratios. For this reason, it is extremely useful to find a way to express Pareto's Law in a quantitative way. A quantitative expression can be used in management systems design as a tool to build into the system the principle of management by exception. Thus, if we can identify the few elements that account for most of the performance in a system, we can design more elaborate controls for them and less elaborate—and cheaper—controls for the majority of the items that account for a small fraction of total performance. In addition, there are many operational applications where a quantitative description of Pareto's Law can be useful, such as the development of preference curves, sales forecasting for fashion items, and the design of inventory and financial systems.

Pareto's Law can best be described graphically. If we sort items in decreasing sequence and plot the cumulative fraction of items on the horizontal axis and the cumulative fraction of contribution that they represent on the vertical axis, we will always obtain a curve with a shape similar to that shown in

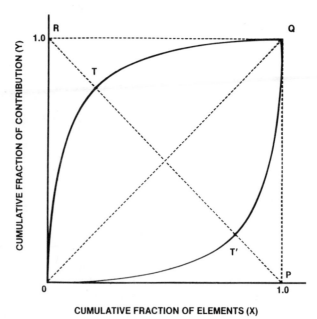

Figure A.1. Analysis by Contribution Curve

Figure A.1, along OTQ. If items are sorted in increasing sequence instead, and their cumulative fractions are plotted on the same scales, we obtain a curve with a shape such as OT'Q. The information needed to plot a curve such as OTQ is shown in a typical report in Table A.1 The actual contribution values of items are sometimes multiplied by a weight, to account for factors not measurable in monetary units, such as criticalness of the item.

2. EXISTING METHODS

Many approaches have been developed to describe this type of distribution analytically. One well-known approach is to use a lognormal distribution to derive an equation to fit the data. This approach is based on the property that generally the logarithms of the contribution values are normally distributed. Thus, we can plot those values against the cumulative fractions of items and contribution using lognormal scales, and we obtain two parallel lines, as shown in Figure A.2.

To compare several lognormal distributions, it is useful to define a measure called *standard ratio*. This is the ratio between the contribution values at the mean plus one standard deviation and at the mean. For a normal distri-

Table A.1. *Analysis by Contribution: Typical Input Data Report Format*

No.	Description	Cumulative Fraction	Value (Dollars)	Weight	Fraction of Total	Cumulative Fraction
1	Bearings 1/8"	.125	108,000	1.00	.3376	.3376
2	Bearings 1"	.250	87,300	1.00	.2729	.6105
3	Valves 1/2"	.375	61,600	1.00	.1926	.8031
4	Bearings 1/4"	.500	33,400	1.00	.1044	.9075
5	Valves 1"	.625	21,900	1.00	.0685	.9760
6	Valves 1 1/2"	.750	5,800	1.00	.0181	.9941
7	Bearings 3/4"	.875	1,200	1.00	.0038	.9976
8	Fan belts	1.000	700	1.00	.0021	1.0000
Total			319,900		1.0000	

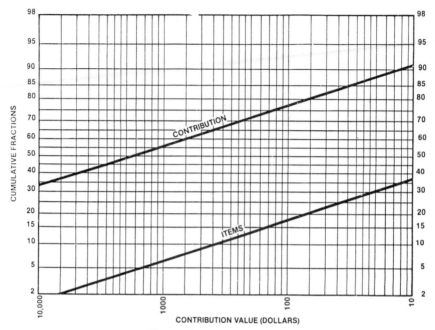

Figure A.2. Lognormal Graph

bution, those values correspond to cumulative fractions of .84 and .50, respectively. If the logarithms of contribution values are normally distributed, the two lines are parallel; therefore, the standard ratio is the same for both contribution and items. As the distribution of the logarithms of contribution values differs from normal, the two lines converge, and therefore the standard ratio of the two lines differs. Under those conditions, it becomes more difficult to compare different distributions.

In a lognormal distribution, the function can be completely described by two parameters: the mean (*m*) and the standard deviation (*s*), by the equation:

$$f(v)dv = \frac{1}{\sqrt{2\pi}\,s}\exp - \left[\frac{(\log_e v - m)^2}{2s^2} \right]\frac{dv}{v} \qquad (1)$$

where *v* is the annual volume of sales for an item. The complexity of this equation makes its analysis and manipulation difficult for most practical applications. Another approach is to use an equation to fit a curve describing the increasing sequence sort of the cumulative data, such as:

$$\frac{X - Y}{\sqrt{2}} = A \left(\frac{X + Y}{\sqrt{2}} \right)^B \left(\sqrt{2} - \frac{X + Y}{\sqrt{2}} \right)^C$$

where:

$$A > 0, \quad B > 0, \quad C > 0$$

This approach, developed by Kakwani and Podder, is somewhat popular in economic analysis. It can be used for other types of analysis and can be converted into a decreasing sequence distribution by the transformation $X = 1 - X$, and $Y = 1 - Y$.

Again, this approach is extremely complicated to use. The alternative is to find a simpler equation that represents the function with good accuracy. There are many simple equations that can represent a curve with a shape such as the one shown in Figure A.1. A common approximation uses Equation (2):

$$Y = X^N \tag{2}$$

Equation (2) is simple and therefore easy to use; however, it produces curves that are not symmetric around axis RP, which is a common property of many real-life curves, and is too steep near 0 for most practical applications.

3. PROPOSED METHOD

Our analysis of a wide variety of management problems has led us to an excellent description of real-life distributions using the equation:

$$Y = \frac{(1 + A)X}{A + X} \tag{3}$$

Given a set of actual points (X_i, Y_i), we can determine the value of A by the least squares method, using the expression:

$$\sum Y_i - (1 + A) \sum \frac{X_i}{A + X_i} = 0 \tag{4}$$

and calculating A by successive approximations.

Once the value of A has been determined, we can define a quantitative characteristic of the curve that allows us to define uniquely a curve and compare it with other curves. We will call that characteristic *steepness* (*S*), and we will define it as the ratio between two areas in Figure A.1:

$$S = \frac{\text{area between curve OTQ and diagonal OQ}}{\text{area of triangle OQR}}$$

Thus, we see that maximum steepness is attained when the curve coincides with lines ORQ and $S=1$. Minimum steepness is attained when the curve coincides with diagonal OQ and $S=0$. Therefore, in all practical cases we will have:

$$0 < S < 1$$

To calculate S, we first find area M_1 under OTQ:

$$M_1 = \int_0^1 \frac{(1 + A)X}{A + X} \, dx$$

$$= (1 + A)\left(1 + A \log_e \frac{A}{1 + A}\right)$$

Since OP=1, this area also represents the value of the average contribution (Y) of the elements in the set. Subtracting from M_1 the area of triangle OPQ $= 1/2$, we obtain the area M between the curve OTQ and the diagonal OQ:

$$M = (1 + A)\left(1 + A \log_e \frac{A}{1 + A}\right) - \frac{1}{2}$$

and we obtain the steepness S of the curve by dividing M by the area of triangle OQR $= 1/2$, thus we have:

$$S = 2(1 + A)\left(1 + A \log_e \frac{A}{1 + A}\right) - 1 \tag{5}$$

Several other properties of the curve can be established from Equation (3).

4.   PROPERTIES OF THE FUNCTION

4.1.   Determining the Point of Diminishing Returns

A useful characteristic of the distribution is its point of diminishing returns. This can be calculated by setting the derivative of the curve's equation equal to 1:

$$\frac{dy}{dx} = \frac{1 + A}{A + x}\left(1 - \frac{x}{A + x}\right) = 1$$

From there we obtain:

$$X_D = \sqrt{A(1 + A)} - A$$

$$Y_D = \frac{(1 + A)\left[\sqrt{A(1 + A)} - A\right]}{\sqrt{A(1 + A)}}$$

which are the coordinates of the point of diminishing returns. It can be easily demonstrated that this point is the intersection of curve OTQ with diagonal RP, and also the point where $X + Y = 1$.

4.2. Dividing the ABC Curve into Three Sectors

We can divide the curve into three sectors A, B, C such that those items in Sector A are few but account for most of total contribution, those in Sector B account for the same contribution as their fraction of items, and those in Sector C are such that they account for a large fraction of total items, but a small fraction of total contribution. A simple way to divide the curve in that fashion is to define the characteristics of the intermediate Sector B. For example, if we want to divide the curve in such a way that items in Sector B account for a fraction F of both total items and total contribution, we can calculate the coordinates of points (X_1, Y_1) and (X_2, Y_2) that separate Sectors A, B and C by using Equation (3) with the conditions $X_2 - X_1 = Y_2 - Y_1 = F$, and we obtain:

$$X_1 = \sqrt{\left(\frac{2A + F}{2}\right)^2 + A(1 - F)} - \frac{2A + F}{2}$$

$$X_2 = X_1 + F$$

The values of Y_1 and Y_2 can be calculated from Equation (3), by replacing X with X_1 and X_2, respectively. As a rule of thumb, $F = .9X_D + .05$ gives a good sectioning of the curve.

4.3. Recalculating the Equation of a Partial ABC Curve

Given Equation (3), if we want to retain only the first m of the items, and delete the remaining $(1 - m)$ of them, we can calculate the new equation of the remaining items by the following substitutions in Equation (3):

$$mX \text{ for } X$$

and

$$Y \frac{(1 + A)m}{A + m} \text{ for } Y$$

Thus, we obtain the equation of the resulting curve as a function of A and m:

$$Y = \frac{(1 + A)mX}{A + mX} \cdot \frac{A + m}{(1 + A)m}$$

therefore:

$$Y = \frac{(A + m)X}{A + mX}$$

From Equation (3), we have:

$$A = \frac{X(1 - Y)}{Y - X}$$

and replacing the value of Y just found, we can calculate the new coefficient A', which describes the curve directly:

$$A' = \frac{X \left[1 - \dfrac{(A + m)X}{A + mX} \right]}{\dfrac{(A + m)X}{A + mX} - X}$$

therefore: $A' = \dfrac{A}{m}$

With this value, we can describe the new curve replacing it in Equation (3), and we can calculate the new steepness, by replacing it in Equation (5).

4.4. Resorting the ABC Curve

Given quation (3), representing the set of items sorted in decreasing sequence, we can easily calculate the equation of the same set of items sorted in increasing sequence by the transformations $Y = 1 - Y$ and $X = 1 - X$ in

Equation (3), and thus we obtain:

$$Y = \frac{AX}{1 + A - X}$$

and we can determine the new steepness S' as:

$$S' = 1 - 2A \left[(1 + A) \log_e \frac{1 + A}{A} - 1 \right]$$

Appendix B

Technique to Fit a Polygonal Approximation to Nonlinear Functions

In most practical operational problems, it is necessary to consider nonlinear cost equations. Such equations describe total cost as a function of activity level. Activity level can be expressed in physical units—such as tons or gallons—and in time units—such as hours or days. Cost equations may represent processes showing economies of scale and diseconomies of scale beyond a point, or processes with economies of scale alone. When a cost function must include both economies and diseconomies of scale, it is practical to use a cubic parabola with an inflexion point to describe it. When a cost function includes only economies of scale, additional accuracy may be gained by using an exponential relationship. In both cases, it is generally necessary to find a set of linear functions to approximate the curve. This requirement is common in models using linear programming and similar techniques. This appendix presents a methodology to approximate the two types of curves mentioned, by means of polygons.

1. APPROXIMATING AN EXPONENTIAL FUNCTION

An exponential function is of the type:

$$Y = A + BX^N \tag{1}$$

where
X = activity level
Y = total cost
A, B, N = constants calculated by regression.

Given a curve such as the one in Equation (1), we can develop a polygonal approximation as described in the following sections.

1.1. Calculate the Best Fitting Initial Line

First, we select a range of activity where the solution is most likely to lie, or where normal activity takes place, and replace the curve by a straight line that meets two conditions within that range:

1. The surface under the curve is equal to the surface under the line.
2. The error between the costs calculated on the curve and on the line, at the boundaries, are equal.

Given a cost equation such as Equation (1), and a range between a lower boundary $X = l$, and a higher boundary $X = h$, the surface under the curve is:

$$S_c = \int_l^h (A + BX)dx = A(h - l) + \frac{B}{N + 1} (h^{N+1} - l^{N+1}) \qquad (2)$$

The surface under a line with equation $Y = K + LX$ in the same range is:

$$S_L = \int_l^h (K + LX)dx = K(h - l) + \frac{1}{2} L(h^2 - l^2) \qquad (3)$$

Since $S_c = S_L$, we have:

$$L = \frac{2\left[(A - K)(h - l) + \dfrac{B}{N + 1} (h^{N+1} - l^{N+1})\right]}{h^2 - l^2}$$

If we define the error E_i at a boundary as:

$$E_i = \frac{Y_l - Y_c}{Y_c} \qquad (4)$$

where Y_l = ordinate on the line for $X = i$
$\quad\ Y_c$ = ordinate on the curve for $X = i$

We have:

$$E_l = \frac{K + Ll - A - Bl^N}{A + Bl^N} \qquad (5)$$

and:

$$E_h = \frac{K + Lh - A - Bh^N}{A + Bh^N} \qquad (6)$$

and since the second condition is:

$$E_l = E_h$$

we have:

$$L = \frac{BK(h^N - l^N)}{A(h - l) - Bhl(h^{N-1} - l^{N-1})} \tag{7}$$

And since Equations (4) and (7) represent L, their right-hand sides are equal, therefore:

$$K = \frac{2[A(h - l) - Bhl(h^{N-1} - l^{N-1})]\left[A(h - l) + \dfrac{B}{N + 1}(h^{N+1} - l^{N+1})\right]}{(h - l)\{B(h^N - l^N)(h + l) + 2[A(h - l) - Bhl(h^{N-1} - l^{N-1})]\}} \tag{8}$$

Thus, we can calculate K with Equation (8), and then L, with Equation (7), which define the line that replaces the curve in range (l, h). For example, given the curve with equation $Y = 2 + 3X^{.5}$ plotted in Figure B.1, we can select the range $(3, 11)$ and we have:

$$A = 2$$
$$B = 3$$
$$N = .5$$
$$l = 3$$
$$h = 11$$

replacing those values in Equation (8), we have:

$$K = 5.554$$

and with this value plus the previous values, we obtain from Equation (7):

$$L = .6095$$

Thus, the line that replaces the curve in range $(3, 11)$ has the equation:

$$Y = 5.554 + .6095X \tag{9}$$

which is plotted in Figure B.1 as segment CD.

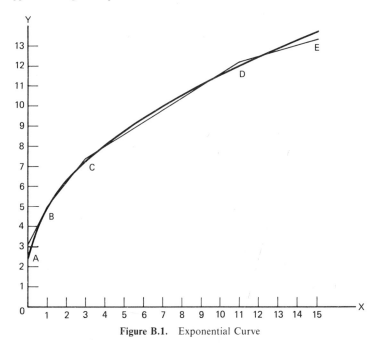

Figure B.1. Exponential Curve

1.2. Calculate the Rest of the Polygon

The next step in the procedure is to calculate the equations of the other lines that constitute the rest of the polygon. The next line to be calculated should be either to the left of $X = 3$, or to the right of $X = 11$. In order to calculate either line, we establish two conditions to be met in the new range to be selected:

1. The surface under the curve and the surface under the line should be equal.
2. The new line should have a common point with the previously fitted line, at the boundary.

If the new line has the equation $Y = P + QX$, then for a range (s, l) we can express the value of Q transforming Equation (4):

$$Q = \frac{2 \left[(A - P)(l - s) + \dfrac{B}{N + 1} (l^{N+1} - s^{N+1}) \right]}{l^2 - s^2} \qquad (10)$$

This value of Q represents the equal surface condition. The second condition is that for $X = l$, the ordinates of the new line and that of the previous line are equal; thus:

$$Y_{\text{new}} = P + Ql \tag{11}$$

$$Y_{\text{prev}} = K + Ll \tag{12}$$

therefore

$$P + Ql = K + Ll$$

and

$$Q = \frac{K - P + Ll}{l} \tag{13}$$

Equating the right-hand sides of Equations (11) and (13), we have:

$$P = \frac{(l - s)[2Al - (l + s)(K + Ll)] + \dfrac{2Bl}{N + 1}(l^{N+1} - s^{N+1})}{(l - s)^2} \tag{14}$$

With Equation (14) we can calculate P; then we can calculate Q with Equation (13).

Continuing with our example, if we select range (1, 3) we have:

$$A = 2$$
$$B = 3$$
$$N = .5$$
$$l = 3$$
$$s = 1$$
$$K = 5.554$$
$$L = .6095$$

Therefore

$$P = 3.824$$

and

$$Q = 1.186$$

Thus, the line that replaces the curve in range $(1, 3)$ is $Y = 3.824 + 1.186X$, shown in Figure B.1 as segment BC.

Next, we can fit a line in range $(0, 1)$, where we have the following values to replace in Equations (14) and (13):

$$A = 2$$
$$B = 3$$
$$N = .5$$
$$l = 1$$
$$s = 0$$
$$K = 3.824$$
$$L = 1.186$$

and we obtain:

$$P = 2.990$$
$$Q = 2.020$$

The line $Y = 2.990 + 2.020X$ is plotted in Figure B.1 as segment AB.

Similarly, we can plot a line to the right of boundary $h = 11$, in range $(11, 15)$ using Equations (14) and (13), with the following values:

$$A = 2$$
$$B = 3$$
$$N = .5$$
$$l = 11$$
$$s = 15$$
$$K = 5.554$$
$$L = .6095$$

and we obtain:

$$P = 9.2478$$
$$Q = .2737$$

The line $Y = 9.2478 + .2737X$ is plotted in Figure B.1 as segment DE. This line completes the polygon $ABCDE$ in range $(0, 15)$.

2. FITTING AND APPROXIMATING A CUBIC PARABOLA WITH AN INFLEXION POINT

Given the equation of a cubic parabola:

$$Y = A + BX + CX^2 + DX^3$$

it will have a point of inflexion if its first two derivatives are equal to 0:

$$\frac{dy}{dx} = B + 2CX + 3DX^2 = 0 \tag{1}$$

$$\frac{d^2y}{dx^2} = C + 3DX = 0 \tag{2}$$

From Equation (2), we can determine that the point of inflexion will be at:

$$x = -\frac{C}{3D} \tag{3}$$

Replacing this value in Equation (1):

$$B - \frac{2C^2}{3D} + \frac{C^2}{3D} = 0$$

therefore

$$B = \frac{C^2}{3D} \tag{4}$$

Thus, the equation of a cubic parabola having an inflexion point at $X = -\frac{C}{3D} = I$ can be expressed as:

$$Y = A + \frac{C^2}{3D}X + CX^2 + DX^3$$

or

$$Y = A - ICX + CX^2 + DX^3 \tag{5}$$

where $I > 0$ is the abscissa of the inflexion point.

Given a set of N points along such a curve, we can determine the values of A, C, and D by the least squares method, using the equations

$$\Sigma Y = AN - C(I\Sigma X - \Sigma X^2) + D\Sigma X^3 \tag{6}$$

$$\Sigma XY = A\Sigma X + C(I\Sigma X^2 - \Sigma X^3) + D\Sigma X^4 \tag{7}$$

$$\Sigma X^2 Y = A\Sigma X^2 - C(I\Sigma X^3 - \Sigma X^4) + D\Sigma X^5 \tag{8}$$

where I is an input. If I is not given, it can be replaced by $-\frac{C}{3D}$, and the values of A, C, and D can be calculated from the same set of equations. For example, if $I = 5$, and the following points are given:

X	0	1	2	3	4	6	7	8	9	10
Y	2.0	3.0	3.6	3.9	4.0	4.2	4.4	4.7	5.3	6.0

then using Equations (6), (7), and (8), we can obtain:

$$A = 2$$
$$C = -.25$$
$$D = .0167$$

And using Equation (3), we can verify that the point of inflexion will be at:

$$X = - \frac{-.25}{3 \times .0167} = 4.990$$

which is close enough to the input value $I = 5$. This curve is shown in Figure B.2.

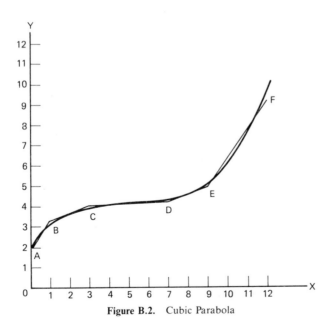

Figure B.2. Cubic Parabola

2.1. Approximating the Curve with a Polygon

Given the curve in Equation (5):

$$Y = A - ICX + CX^2 + DX^3$$

we can approximate it with a polygon, as described in the following sections.

2.2. Calculate the Best Fitting Initial Line

In a range (l, h) selected, we can calculate the coefficients of the best fitting line using two conditions:

1. The areas under the curve and under the line will be equal.
2. The errors at the boundaries will be equal.

If the line sought has the equation $Y = K + LX$, then the area under it in the range (l, h) will be:

$$S_l = \int_l^h (K + LX)dX = K(h - l) + \frac{L}{2}(h^2 - l^2)$$

and the area under the curve in Equation (5) in the same range will be:

$$S_c = \int_l^h (A - ICX + CX^2 + DX^3)dX$$

$$= A(h - l) - \frac{1}{2} IC(h^2 - l^2) + \frac{1}{3}C(h^3 - l^3)$$

$$+ \frac{1}{4}D(h^4 - l^4)$$

And since $S_l = S_c$, we have:

$$K = A - \frac{1}{2}IC(h + l) + \frac{1}{3}C\,\frac{h^3 - l^3}{h - l} + \frac{1}{4}D\,\frac{h^4 - l^4}{h - l}$$

$$- \frac{1}{2}L(h + l) \tag{9}$$

To introduce the second condition, we will define the error between the line and the curve at a given point as:

$$E_i = \frac{Y_l - Y_c}{Y_c}$$

where Y_l = ordinate on the line for $X = i$
Y_c = ordinate on the curve for $X = i$

Thus we have:

$$E_l = \frac{K + Ll - A + ICl - Cl^2 - Dl^3}{A - ICl + Cl^2 + Dl^3}$$

$$E_h = \frac{K + Lh - A + ICh - Ch^2 - Dh^3}{A - ICh + Ch^2 + Dh^3}$$

To simplify these expressions, let us define

$$t = A - ICl + Cl^2 + Dl^3 \tag{10}$$

$$u = A - ICh + Ch^2 + Dh^3 \tag{11}$$

$$v = A - \frac{1}{2}IC(h + l) + \frac{1}{3}C\frac{h^3 - l^3}{h - l} + \frac{1}{4}D\frac{h^4 - l^4}{h - l} \tag{12}$$

and since $E_l = E_h$:

$$K = \frac{L(ht - lu)}{u - t} \tag{13}$$

And from Equations (9) and (13):

$$L = \frac{2v(u - t)}{(h - l)(u + t)} \tag{14}$$

Given the cubic parabola in the example, with equation

$$Y = 2 + 1.25X - .25X^2 + .0167X^3$$

and $I = 5$, we can calculate the best fitting line in the range $(3, 7)$ as follows: first we calculate t, u, and v from Equations (10), (11), and (12) and obtain:

$$t = 3.951$$
$$u = 4.228$$
$$v = 4.088$$

Replacing those values in Equations (14) and (13), we obtain:

$$L = .0692$$

and

$$K = 3.741$$

and the best fitting line in range (3, 7) is $Y = 3.741 + .0692X$, shown in Figure B.2 as segment CD.

2.3. Calculate the Rest of the Polygon

Once the first side of the polygon has been fitted in range (l, h), we can fit the next side of the polygon either to the left of l or to the right of h by imposing two conditions for the new line to meet:

1. It must have a common point at the boundary with the line previously fitted.
2. In the new range selected, the area under the line must equal that under the curve.

If the line sought has the equation $Y = P + QX$, then for $X = l$, the first condition will be met if:

$$P + Ql = K + Ll$$

therefore

$$P = K + l(L - Q) \tag{15}$$

and in range (s, l), the second condition will be met if:

$$P(l - s) + \frac{Q}{2}(l^2 - s^2) = A(l - s) - \frac{1}{2}IC(l^2 - s^2)$$

$$+ \frac{1}{3}C(l^3 - s^3) + \frac{1}{4}D(l^4 - s^4)$$

Therefore:

$$P = A - \frac{1}{2}IC(l + s) + \frac{1}{3}C\frac{l^3 - s^3}{l - s} + \frac{1}{4}D\frac{l^4 - s^4}{l - s}$$

$$- \frac{1}{2}Q(l + s) \tag{16}$$

and designating:

$$w = A - \frac{1}{2}IC(l + s) + \frac{1}{3}C\frac{l^3 - s^3}{l - s} + \frac{1}{4}D\frac{l^4 - s^4}{l - s}$$

we have from Equations (15) and (16):

$$K + l(L - Q) = w - \frac{1}{2}Q(l + s)$$

from where we obtain:

$$Q = \frac{2(K + Ll - w)}{l - s} \tag{17}$$

Using Equations (17) and (16), we can then calculate Q and P, respectively. For example, in range (1, 3) we have:

$$
\begin{aligned}
K &= 3.741 \\
L &= .0692 \\
l &= 3 \\
s &= 1 \\
A &= 2 \\
C &= -.25 \\
D &= .0167 \\
I &= 5
\end{aligned}
$$

Therefore

$$w = 3.584$$

and

$$Q = .3646$$
$$P = 2.855$$

and the polygon side in range (1, 3) is defined by equation $Y = 2.855 + .3646X$, shown in Figure B.2 as segment BC.

The same approach can be used to fit additional sides of the polygon either to the left of s or to the right of h by using Equations (17) and (15) repeatedly, replacing K and L with the latest values of P and Q for the adjacent segment. For example, in range (0, 1) we have:

$$K = 2.855$$
$$L = .3646$$
$$l = 1$$
$$s = 0$$
$$A = 2$$
$$C = -.25$$
$$D = .0167$$
$$I = 5$$

Therefore

$$w = 2.546$$

and

$$Q = 1.347$$
$$P = 1.873$$

Thus, the best fitting line in range $(0, 1)$ is $Y = 1.873 + 1.347X$, shown in Figure B.2 as segment AB.

Similarly, in range $(7, 9)$ we have:

$$K = 3.741$$
$$L = .0692$$
$$l = 7$$
$$s = 9$$
$$A = 2$$
$$C = -.25$$
$$D = .0167$$
$$I = 5$$

Therefore

$$w = 4.601$$

and

$$Q = .3756$$
$$P = 1.596$$

Thus, the best fitting line in range $(7, 9)$ is $Y = 1.596 + .3756X$, shown in Figure B.2 as segment DE.

Finally, for range (9, 12) we have:

$$K = 1.596$$
$$L = .3756$$
$$l = 9$$
$$s = 12$$
$$A = 2$$
$$C = -.25$$
$$D = .0167$$
$$I = 5$$

Therefore

$$w = 7.102$$

and

$$Q = 1.417$$
$$P = -7.777$$

Thus, the best fitting line in range (9, 12) is $Y = -7.777 + 1.417X$, shown in Figure B.2 as segment EF, completing the polygon in range (0, 12).

It is important to notice that although there are always errors introduced by using a polygonal approximation, such errors can be controlled. This is done by using larger or smaller ranges, and therefore fewer or more sides on the polygon. The higher the number of sides used to form the polygon, the smaller the errors will be, and vice versa.

Finally, we can point out that the method described here is general enough to be used with any other nonlinear functions that must be approximated by a polygon, or any curve segment that must be replaced by a straight line, ensuring best fit.

Appendix C

Methodology to Develop Information System Specifications

To develop the specifications of an information system, we start from an informational map such as that shown in Figure 32. There we see an abridged example of the life cycle for the human resource "employees." Similar maps can be prepared for all other resources.

The mapping technique relates organizational functions to the processes involved in the life cycle of each resource. The relationship is established by the concatenations of the five elements that define management: decisions, actions, events, results, and terminals.

As previously discussed, the management process can be described as an interaction between decision makers in an organization and the environment surrounding them. Their interaction can be illustrated, from an informational point of view, as in Figure C.1, which shows the management cycle in summary form. There we see that changes resulting from external and internal events are represented as *data* collected and are translated into a fashion suitable for automated processing.

Data are compiled into data bases, where they are available to information *systems* that can process them and transform them into information for decision and action support.

Systems provide information to decision makers that constitute well-defined organizational units, which we shall call *organisms*. In them, managers internalize information, add it to their knowledge, and make decisions; these lead to actions, which in turn create additional changes that are again represented by data.

From the outline above, we see that we can describe the management process—from an informational point of view—in terms of the confluence of three entities: *data, systems,* and *organisms.* When these interact, management functions take place.

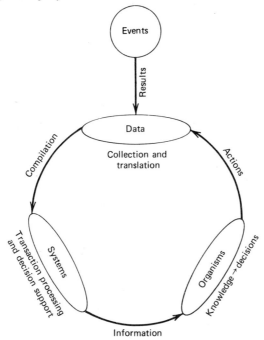

Figure C.1 The management cycle

To specify the characteristics of an information system, we need to describe the management process in detail. This can be accomplished by focusing on the elemental components of the management process, which we shall define as *management vectors*.

A management vector can be described as a triad whose dimensions are data, systems, and organisms. This concept is illustrated in Figure C.2.

Thus we can define any of the management elements in an informational map as a *set* of management vectors. And we can define a management function as a set of management elements, or a superset of management vectors.

To apply these concepts in practice, it is necessary to define units of measure for each of the three dimensions of a management vector. To do so, we can define a set of two-dimensional vectors for each dimension of the management vector. In each case, the *resources* affected by the management vector constitute one of the two dimensions.

From a practical point of view, it is convenient to define the resources affected by each management vector in some detail. The matrices in Tables C.1, C.2, and C.3 show a classification that works well in practice; in some cases, some of the resources shown may be detailed further. It is convenient

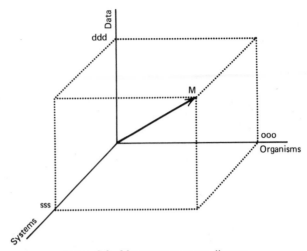

Figure C.2 Management vector diagram

to number all resources with a two-digit number as shown, so that, for example, 10 represents any physical resource, 11 represents only land, and so on.

Because each of the three dimensions of a management vector has two dimensions itself, we must define one more dimension for each of them. This can be done as shown in Tables C.1, C.2, and C.3. There we have defined three matrices, each having one row for every resource and one column for every element characterizing that particular dimension.

From the first matrix we can derive the two-dimensional vectors that define all data to be considered. These can be identified by three-digit labels. For example, a datum representing a facility-related transaction can be designated 123; a datum representing financial constraints, 208, and so on.

Similarly, from the second matrix we can derive the two-dimensional vectors that define all systems to be considered. These can also be identified by three-digit labels. For example, a system representing the processing of income data can be designated 242; a system representing simulation of the behavior of informational resources, 405, and so on.

Finally, from the third matrix, we can derive the two-dimensional vectors that define all organisms to be considered. These can also be identified by three-digit labels. For example, an operational, line organism dealing with customers—such as a sales force—can be identified as 328; a tactical, staff organism dealing with hardware—such as a group of telecommunications planners—can be identified as 433, and so on.

With the definitions we have given, we can construct management vectors of three dimensions representing data, systems, and organisms. Such vectors

Table C.1 Data Classification Matrix

Data Classes

Resource Classes	0. Entities			4. Relationships	5. Attributes				
	1. Objects	2. Agents	3. Transactions		6. Physical	7. Financial	8. Constraints	9. Conditions	
10. *Physical*									
11. Land									
12. Facilities			123						
13. Equipment									
14. Materials									
15. Energy									
20. *Financial*							208		
21. Assets									
22. Liabilities									
23. Equity									
24. Income									
25. Expenses									
30. *Human*									
31. Prospects									
32. Customers									
33. Suppliers									
34. Employees									
35. Competitors									
36. Owners									
37. Public									
40. *Informational*									
41. Data									
42. Knowledge									
43. Hardware									
44. Software									
50. *Time*									
51. Date									
52. Period									

203

Table C.2 *Systems Classification Matrix*

	Systems Classes					
	1. Transaction Processing			4. Decision Support		
Resource Classes		2. Processing	3. Reporting		5. Simulation	6. Inquiry
10. *Physical*						
11. Land						
12. Facilities						
13. Equipment						
14. Materials						
15. Energy						
20. *Financial*						
21. Assets						
22. Liabilities						
23. Equity						
24. Income		242				
25. Expenses						
30. *Human*						
31. Prospects						
32. Customers						
33. Suppliers						
34. Employees						
35. Competitors						
36. Owners						
37. Public						
40. *Informational*					405	
41. Data						
42. Knowledge						
43. Hardware						
44. Software						
50. *Time*						
51. Date						
52. Period						

Table C.3 *Organisms Classification Matrix*

| | Organisms Classes | | | | | |
| | 1. Staff | | | 5. Line | | |
Resource Classes	2. Strategic	3. Tactical	4. Operational	6. Strategic	7. Tactical	8. Operational
10. *Physical*						
11. Land						
12. Facilities						
13. Equipment						
14. Materials						
15. Energy						
20. *Financial*						
21. Assets						
22. Liabilities						
23. Equity						
24. Income						
25. Expenses						
30. *Human*						
31. Prospects						
32. Customers						328
33. Suppliers						
34. Employees						
35. Competitors						
36. Owners						
37. Public						
40. *Informational*						
41. Data						
42. Knowledge						
43. Hardware		433				
44. Software						
50. *Time*						
51. Date						
52. Period						

can be identified by a nine-digit label of the form *ddd-sss-ooo*, where *ddd* represents the two-dimensional data vector, and *sss*, and *ooo* the similar systems and organisms vectors.

With those elements, we can use an informational map, such as the one in Figure 32, to define the management vectors of each entity. To facilitate the analysis, it is useful to identify each entity; we can do that by designating each function by a two-digit number, and within each function we can number all entities consecutively from top to bottom with another two-digit number. Thus each entity in an informational map is uniquely identified by a four-digit label. For example, for the Functional Management function in Figure 32 the decision needed to determine whether personnel needs are satisfied or not can be labeled 0102, and so on.

For each element in the informational map we can now identify the set of management vectors that define it. Following that procedure, we can define all the management vectors composing the resource administration processes of an organization.

Once all management vectors are defined, we can input them into an automated data base. Then we can sort them and compile them in any fashion of interest to establish the characteristics of the information systems needed to support the management process.

Typically, it is useful to start with a sort on systems as major key, organisms as intermediate key, and data as minor key, as shown in Table C.4. Such a sort provides a picture of the components of each elemental system. Then several elemental systems may be combined, forming more complex

Table C.4 *Management Vector Sort*

System	Organism	Data	Vector
100	101	101	0203
100	103	105	0207
100	107	109	0817
100	113	127	1503
100	113	129	1521
103	104	108	0311
103	104	112	0331
103	109	221	0714
103	117	341	1226
212	403	322	1401
⋮	⋮	⋮	⋮

system specifications. Additional sorts may be made to evaluate the requirements of clusters of organisms and data.

The main advantage of this methodology is that it allows the analyst to develop specifications using the computer to compile and sort all data; this makes the approach fast and practical. Another advantage of this methodology is its universality: it can be applied to any type of organization.

Annotated Bibliography

INTRODUCTION

1. The Economic Environment

Attali, Jacques. *Les Trois Mondes*. Paris: Fayard, 1981.

A humanistic analysis of the current world crisis, describing three aspects of reality: exchange and regulation, production, and organization. With a personal view on how to approach the problems confronting the world.

Ayers, Robert U. *Uncertain Futures*. New York: Wiley, 1979.

An overall technical examination of past and future sociopolitical and economic developments, including scenarios of possible critical developments.

Brandt, Willy (Chairman). *North–South: A Program for Survival*. Cambridge, Mass.: The MIT Press, 1980.

A report prepared by 18 members of different countries, containing recommendations on international economic and political issues, to help resolve the problems between developed and developing countries.

Colinvaux, Robert. *The Fates of Nations*. New York: Simon and Schuster, 1980.

An analysis of history from a biological point of view, resulting in the identification of basic principles that seem to govern the behavior of human groups and their interactions.

Crozier, Michel. *Le Mal Americain*. Paris: Fayard, 1980.

A sociologist's evaluation of the factors underlying the social and economic problems America confronts. Concludes with a discussion of lessons to guide Europe's reaction to their situation.

de Saint Phalle, Thibaut. *Trade, Inflation, and the Dollar*. New York: Oxford University Press, 1981.

Describes America's economic decline since World War II and the reasons behind it. Places especial emphasis on the lack of international perspective of successive U.S. administrations and their subordination of international financial matters to the needs of domestic politics.

Drucker, Peter F. *Managing in Turbulent Times*. New York: Harper & Row, 1980.

A sweeping, far-reaching review of the issues confronting business in the years ahead. Ranges from analysis on how to adjust for inflation and manage productivity to the demographic changes that are creating an integrated world economy.

208

Fuller, R. Buckminster. *Critical Path*. New York: St. Martin's Press, 1981.

An extremely original description of mankind's development from prehistory to our day. Gives a personal view of the nature of the problems facing us and his prescription on how to cope with the challenges ahead.

Giarini, Orio, and Loubergé, Henri. *La Civilisation Technicienne à la Dérive*. Paris: Dunod, 1979.

An analysis of the sources of Western prosperity, leading to the conclusion that the current economic situation is due to the reaching of diminishing returns in technology. Outlines the changes in values that are deemed necessary to create a new civilization.

Gilder, George. *Wealth and Poverty*. New York: Basic Books, 1981.

An analysis of American social and economic policies from the point of view of supply-side economics. One of the best expositions of the views of that school of thinking.

Guiducci, Roberto. *Un Mondo Capovolto*. Milan: Rizzoli, 1979.

A sociological analysis of the world reality today. Provides an explanation of why neither Marxism nor capitalism focuses on the important elements that characterize today's world society, including changes in political and cultural institutions, workers' organizations, youth problems, and women's liberation.

Hansen, Alvin H. *A Guide to Keynes*. New York: McGraw-Hill, 1953.

A thorough explanation of Keynes's ideas, as presented in his general theory. Contains a number of points where the author corrects some of Keynes's statements and conclusions.

Harris, Marvin. *America Now*. New York: Simon and Schuster, 1981.

An anthropological interpretation of socioeconomic changes that have taken place in American society since World War II. Provides an original view on how such diverse phenomena as rising crime, women's liberation, and the decline in product quality in the United States are related.

Henderson, Hazel. *The Politics of the Solar Age*. Garden City, N.Y.: Anchor Books, 1981.

A futurist's look into the problems of traditional macroeconomic theories, described as politics in disguise, and providing original prescriptions to reorient social organization, and economic policy.

Jantsch, Erich. *The Self-organizing Universe*. New York: Pergamon, 1980.

A humanistic discussion of revolutionary new scientific concepts: self-organization and dissipative structures. Reviews the concept of self-organization as manifested in biological, ecological, social, and cultural structures. On that basis, describes the evolution of the universe at all levels, from cosmic, through biological, to sociocultural.

Keynes, J. M. *General Theory of Employment, Interest, and Money*. New York: Harcourt, Brace, 1936.

The classic exposition of Keynes's theory of macroeconomics. A rather technical exposition of the subject.

Miller, Ronald E. *Revitalizing America*. New York: Simon and Schuster, 1980.

A blueprint for attacking the current economic problems in the United States. The recommendations are directed toward creating new relationships among business, labor, and government domestically and toward creating an environment of cooperation among industrialized, less-developed, and OPEC countries abroad.

Nicolis, G., and Prigogine, Ilya. *Self-organization in Non-Equilibrium Systems*. New York: Wiley, 1977.

A highly technical book discussing one of the most important new scientific theories to emerge in the last four decades. Shows how the stability and permanence of classical physics represents only a restricted aspect of reality. Proposes a new paradigm based on the idea that a central force in nature is evolution, that creates diversification and increasing complexity.

Nora, Simon, and Minc, Alain. *L'Informatisation de la Société*. Paris: La Documentation Française, 1978.

A report to the president of France prepared by two high-level French civil servants. Contains an analysis of the social impact of informational resources and outlines the directions in which the French government could act to channel the process of "informatization" of society.

Pribram, Karl H. "Problems Concerning the Structure of Consciousness." In *Consciousness and the Brain*, edited by Gordon E. Globus, Grover Maxwell, and Irwin Savodnik. New York: Plenum Press, 1976.

A summary exposition of a theory of consciousness, based on a holographic model of the mind. Describes psychological phenomena in terms that can be directly related to holographic memories being developed for computers.

Prigogine, Ilya. *From Being to Becoming*. San Francisco: Freeman, 1980.

A slightly technical exposition of Prigogine's theory of self-organization, or the physics of becoming. Outlines the author's belief that we are currently in the midst of a scientific revolution in which even the meaning of the scientific approach is being reappraised.

Salk, Jonas. *The Survival of the Wisest*. New York: Harper & Row, 1973.

A top expert in biology analyzes the growth of human population along the logistics curve typical of the growth pattern of all biological groups of organisms. Focusing on the fact that human population growth is currently passing through the inflexion point in its growth curve, the author describes the social and psychological implications of such fact.

Tinbergen, Jan, coord. *Reshaping the International Order*. New York: Dutton, 1976.

A report prepared by 21 specialists in different disciplines to provide an answer to the question "What new international order should be recommended to the world's statesmen and social groups, so as to meet to the extent practically and realistically possible, the urgent needs of today's population and the probable needs of future generations?"

Vogel, Ezra F. *Japan as No. 1*. Cambridge, Mass.: Harvard University Press, 1979.

A cogent, far-reaching explanation of the causes behind Japan's industrial success. Based on historical, cultural, and economic analysis, points out how Japan seems to have simultaneously solved the economic as well as the social problems now affecting most other nations.

Wanniski, Jude. *The Way the World Works*. New York: Basic Books, 1978.

Considered as the original exposition of supply-side economics. Tries to outline a theory to explain economic success and failure through history.

2. The Resource Management Concept

Bahke, E., ed. *Materialflusssysteme I, II, & III.* Mainz: Krausskopf Verlag, 1978.

A complete yet simple outline of all aspects of materials management systems.

Bender, Paul S. "Logistic System Design." In *Distribution Handbook*, edited by James F. Robison. New York: The Free Press, 1983.

A summary discussion of the principles and methodology underlying the logistic system design process.

Bender, Paul S. "International Logistics." In *Distribution Handbook*, edited by James R. Robison. New York: The Free Press, 1983.

An outline of the major topics involved in the analysis, design, and operation of international logistic systems.

Bender, Paul S. "International Logistics: Organizing for Profit." *Distribution*, October 1981.

A brief article covering practical aspects of international logistics operations.

Blanchard, Benjamin S. *Logistics Engineering and Management.* Englewood Cliffs, N.J.: Prenctice-Hall, 1974.

A complete technical discussion of logistics engineering techniques, with especial emphasis on the reliability and maintenance aspects of logistics systems.

Hadley, G., and Within, T. M. *Analysis of Inventory Systems.* Englewood Cliffs, N.J.: Prentice-Hall, 1963.

A comprehensive survey of the various types of inventory systems, their characteristics, and quantitative rules governing their behavior.

Isard, Walter. *Location and Space-Economy.* Cambridge, Mass.: The MIT Press, 1956.

An excellent analysis of the importance of geographic location on economic activity. Covers all economic aspects relevant to macro site-location problems.

Marlow, W. H., ed. *Modern Trends in Logistics Research.* Cambridge, Mass.: The MIT Press, 1976.

A complete, concise set of papers surveying the major tools and techniques for logistics system design and operation. Because of its publication date, it is not fully up to date on the state of the art as of 1982.

Schwarz, L. B., ed. *Multi-level Production/Inventory Control Systems: Theory and Practice.* Amsterdam: North-Holland, 1981.

A good survey of the current state of multilevel inventory systems analysis techniques. This is an area of critical importance in the development and operation of large-scale logistic systems.

Taff, Charles A. *Management of Physical Distribution and Transportation.* 6th ed. Homewood, Ill.: Irwin, 1978.

A simple, complete outline of all major aspects of the topics mentioned in the title. Because of its publication date, it is not fully up to date on the impact of deregulation on transportation operations.

THE RESOURCE MANAGEMENT PROCESS

Moder, Joseph, J., and Elmaghraby, Salah E., eds. *Handbook of Operations Research*, vols. 1, 2. New York: Van Nostrand, 1978.

A complete outline of the theories and practical applications of operations research technology.

1. Directional Thinking

Arieti, Silvano. *Creativity*. New York: Basic Books, 1976.

A multifaceted discussion of creativity, ranging from its psychological basis through its manifestations in art, science, religion, and philosophy. Covers the interactions between creativity and the social and cultural characteristics of the environment, the traits distinguishing creative persons, and the neurological principles behind it.

Channon, Derek F., and Jalland, Michael. *Multinational Strategic Planning*. London: Macmillan, 1979.

An overview of different planning techniques of interest in multinational environments. Tries to relate the different techniques to the structure of an enterprise.

de Bono, Edward. *New Think: The Use of Lateral Thinking in the Generation of New Ideas*. New York: Basic Books, 1968.

Approaches the problem of creative thinking as a deliberate way of using the human mind. Relates lateral thinking to logical thinking, as complementary ways to view a problem.

Gordon, William J. J. *Synetics*. New York: Harper & Row, 1961.

Discusses specific techniques for bringing together individual problem solvers into integrated problem stating and solving groups.

King, William R., and Cleland, David I. *Strategic Planning and Policy*. New York: Van Nostrand, 1978.

A complete discussion of the topic, including description of techniques, as well as their applications. Of especial interest is the coverage of the interaction between information systems and corporate strategy.

Osborn, Alex F. *Applied Imagination*. New York: Scribner's, 1967.

A comprehensive discussion of techniques to guide creative thinking in both an individual and a group context.

Porter, Michael E. *Competitive Strategy*. New York: The Free Press, 1980.

An all-encompassing presentation of every important aspect of the analysis, development, and implementation of a competitive strategy.

Quinn, James Brian. *Strategies for Change*. Homewood, Ill.: Irwin, 1980.

An analysis of the factors underlying successful strategies. Based on interviews of more than 50 top-level executives of large corporations.

2. Resource Allocation

Bradley, Stephen R., Hax, Arnoldo C., and Magnanti, Thomas L. *Applied Mathematical Programming.* Reading, Mass.: Addison-Wesley, 1977.

An introductory-level discussion of all major aspects and techniques on the subject. Contains numerous examples to illustrate the applications of each technique.

Dantzig, G. B. *Linear Programming and Extensions.* Princeton, N.J.: Princeton University Press, 1963.

The latest edition of the original work that established the field.

Shapiro, Jeremy F. *Mathematical Programming: Structures and Algorithms.* New York: Wiley, 1979.

A comprehensive, in-depth exposition of all relevant aspects of the topic. Summarizes the state of the art in mathematical programming through a discussion of the characteristics of each technique, the underlying philosophy of the field, and many applications examples.

3. Resource Administration

Bender, Paul S. "Mathematical Modeling of the 20/80 Rule: Theory and Practice." *Journal of Business Logistics* 2 (1981).

Describes a proposed technique to represent mathematically Pareto's Law, and shows examples of its practical applications.

Kaufman, Arnold. *La Science de la Decision.* Paris: Dunod, 1965.

An introduction to Praxeology, the science of decision making, covers the choice of decision-making criteria, the uses of optimization, decision making under risk, under uncertainty, and under sequential requirements.

Raiffa, Howard. *Decision Analysis.* Reading, Mass.: Addison-Wesley, 1968.

An introductory exposition of decision making under risk and uncertainty, utility theory, the uses of sampling to support the decision-making process, and group decision making.

Raiffa, Howard, and Schlaifer, Robert. *Applied Statistical Decision Theory.* Cambridge, Mass.: The MIT Press, 1961.

A complete exposition of the mathematical basis of decision theory. Places especial emphasis on the use of experimentation to obtain information to guide the decision maker.

Schlaifer, Robert. *Probability and Statistics for Business Decisions.* New York: McGraw-Hill, 1959.

A comprehensive yet simple exposition of the principles and practical applications of probability theory and statistical analysis to business problems.

RESOURCE MANAGEMENT SYSTEMS

1. Informational Resources

Cherry, Colin. *On Human Communication*. 2d ed. Cambridge, Mass.: The MIT Press, 1966.

A relatively nontechnical survey of the many aspects involved in informational resources, including cybernetics, linguistics, psychology, semantics, phonetics, as well as the statistical characteristics underlying them.

Shannon, Claude E., and Weaver, Warren. *The Mathematical Theory of Communication*. Urbana, Ill.: University of Illinois Press, 1949.

A book of major importance, containing Shannon's historic paper on communication theory, plus Weaver's description of the major ideas in it, in nontechnical language.

von Neumann, John. *The Computer and the Brain*. New Haven, Conn.: Yale University Press, 1958.

The great mathematician who originated the concept of stored program machines describes the similarities between the structures of computing machines and the human brain.

Wiener, Norbert. *Cybernetics*. 2d ed. Cambridge, Mass.: The MIT Press, 1961.

One of the classics of science, which sets the foundations for the understanding and design of computing machines, as well as the description of thinking processes in the human brain.

Zand, Dale E. *Information, Organization and Power*. New York: McGraw-Hill, 1981.

A succinct, stimulating discussion of the implications of the increasingly informational content of managerial functions.

2. Development of an Information System

Bender, Paul S. "Measuring the Value of Automated Decision Support Systems." In *The Economics of Information Processing*, edited by Robert Goldberg and Harold Lorin. New York: Wiley, 1982.

A paper outlining an approach to measure the value obtained from the use of information systems to support the decision-making process.

Date, C. J. *An Introduction to Database Systems*. Reading, Mass.: Addison-Wesley, 1975.

An introductory survey of the main concepts behind database structures and their use.

Gane, Chris, and Sarson, Trish. *Structured Systems Analysis: Tools and Techniques*. Englewood Cliffs, N.J.: Prentice-Hall, 1979.

A detailed description of a technique for systems analysis, including data flow diagrams, development of data dictionaries, structuring an information system, and implementing the technique.

Hartman, W. H., Matthes, H., and Proeme, A. *Management Information Systems Handbook*. New York: McGraw-Hill, 1968.

A comprehensive, practical guide to all aspects of design, development, implementation, and evaluation of information systems.

Keen, Peter G. W., and Morton, Michael S. Scott. *Decision Support Systems: An Organizational Perspective*. Reading, Mass.: Addison-Wesley, 1978.

A complete nontechnical outline of the topic. Presents a clear discussion of the different aspects of the subject, including models of decision making, the decision and implementation process for decision support systems, and methods of evaluation of their benefits.

Martin, James. *Design and Strategy for Distributed Data Processing*. Englewood Cliffs, N.J.: Prentice-Hall, 1981.

A detailed exposition of the principles and tools of design for distributed data processing systems. Includes analysis of distributed data bases and security and auditability of distributed systems.

Miller, James Grier. *Living Systems*. New York: McGraw-Hill, 1978.

An encyclopedic work integrating approaches from many disciplines, to describe the nature and workings of biological and social systems, from the living cell to the world society. Contains especially interesting descriptions of the psychological basis of human reactions to informational loads, the effect of negative feedback on the behavior of living organisms, the characteristics of system and subsystem processes, and the use of models to describe supranational systems.

Orlicky, Joseph. *The Successful Computer System*. New York: McGraw-Hill, 1969.

A comprehensive, nontechnical discussion of the principles of planning, developing, implementing and using computer systems. Written from a managerial standpoint.

Vetter, M., and Maddison, R. N. *Database Design Methodology*. Englewood Cliffs, N.J.: Prentice-Hall, 1981.

A complete technical discussion of the main aspects of database design.

3. Implementation Guidelines

Ewing, David W. *The Human Side of Planning*. New York: Macmillan, 1969.

A cogent, succinct book, describing the techniques used for corporate planning and the role that human factors play in their successes or failures.

Fisher, Roger, and Ury, William. *Getting to Yes*. Boston: Houghton Mifflin, 1981.

Outlines in a clear manner the main principles of successful negotiating. Full of practical advice, focuses on real-life situations, in a serious manner.

Maccoby, Michael. *The Gamesman*. New York: Simon and Schuster, 1976.

Based on interviews with 250 managers from 12 companies, this book contains a readable, practical description of personality traits commonly found in businessmen. Helpful in understanding the personality and motivation of different individuals.

McCarthy, John J. *Why Managers Fail.* . . . New York: McGraw-Hill, 1978.

A practical book dealing with common problems in handling people that can interfere with successful management.

Tarr, Graham. *The Management of Problem Solving.* London: Macmillan, 1973.

A book dealing with the nontechnical, human factors involved in problem-solving situations. Places especial emphasis on the work of groups working on common projects.

4. Implementation of Resource Allocation Systems

Bender, Paul S., Northup, William D., and Shapiro, Jeremy F. "Practical Modeling for Resource Management." *Harvard Business Review*, March–April, 1981.

An article outlining a case study of development and implementation of large-scale optimization systems for resource allocation. Used at strategic, tactical, and operational levels, the paper focuses on the characteristics of the system, practical implementation considerations, and benefits obtained.

Brown, R. W., Northup, W. D., and Shapiro, J. F. *LOGS: An Optimization System for Logistics Planning.* Cambridge, Mass.: Operations Research Center, Massachusetts Institute of Technology, 1981.

A paper describing a general model-generating language representing the state of the art in generation of large-scale models for resource allocation problems.

Demski, Joel S., and Feltham, Gerald A. *Cost Determination.* Ames, Iowa: Iowa State University Press, 1976.

A comprehensive examination of cost structures needed to represent real-life situations in the context of decision support systems.

IBM Corporation. *Logistics Modeling System Using IBM's MPSX/370 at International Paper.* Application Brief GK20–1341–0, 1980.

A short description of the use of MPSX/370 as an optimization tool to solve large-scale logistics problems. Presents practical aspects of specific situations, users' comments on the technology used, and examples of benefits accrued.

5. Implementation of Resource Administration Systems

Buffa, Elwood S., and Taubert, William H. *Production–Inventory Systems: Planning and Control.* Homewood, Ill.: Irwin, 1972.

A complete, practical outline of the basic principles of production management and their relationship to inventory management.

Bussmann, Karl F., and Mertens, Peter. *Operations Research und Datenverarbeitung bei der Produktionsplanung.* Stuttgart: Poeschel Verlag, 1968.

A comprehensive description of the techniques available for automated production planning. Highly technical, but with a practical approach.

Cascio, Wayne F., and Awad, Elias M. *Human Resources Management: An Information Systems Approach.* Reston, Va.: Reston, 1981.

A complete description of human resources management, restricted to the personnel aspects of the function. Describes the major processes involved and their informational representation.

Chen, Peter P., ed. *Entity–Relationship Approach to Systems Analysis and Design.* Amsterdam: North-Holland, 1980.

The Proceedings of the International Conference on Entity–Relationship Approach to Systems Analysis and Design. Contains a wealth of papers on most aspects of the application of Chen's technique.

Copeland, Thomas E., and Weston, J. Fred. *Financial Theory and Corporate Policy.* Reading, Mass.: Addison-Wesley, 1979.

A modern up-to-date book on financial policy, using the latest tools of analysis. Reflects the convergence of microeconomic theory and corporate finance, through the use of such concepts as utility theory, mean–variance theory, and option pricing theory.

Elmaghraby, Salah E. *The Design of Production Systems.* New York: Reinhold, 1966.

A complete review of the theories of optimization of constrained and unconstrained systems as they apply to the design of integrated production systems.

Holt, Charles C., Modigiani, Franco, Muth, John F., and Simon, Herbert A. *Planning Production Inventories, and Work Force.* Englewood Cliffs, N.J.: Prentice-Hall, 1960.

A pioneering work, describing the use of quantitative techniques for the aggregate planning of physical and human resources.

Kotler, Philip. *Marketing Management.* 4th ed. Englewood Cliffs, N.J.: Prentice-Hall, 1980.

A complete survey of the field, outlining the major problems and techniques available to solve them.

6. Organizational Consequences

Charnes, A., Cooper, W. W., and Niehaus, R. J., eds. *Management Science Approaches to Manpower Planning and Organization Design.* New York: North Holland, 1978.

A far-reaching collection of papers on the topic. Of especial interest is that the editors' approach has focused on the interactions between manpower planning and organization design.

Cyert, Richard M., and March, James G. *A Behavioral Theory of the Firm.* Englewood Cliffs, N.J.: Prentice-Hall, 1963.

A ground-breaking book, outlining how behavioral science can be applied in practice to contribute to the solution of organizational decision-making problems.

Dessler, Gary. *Organizational Theory.* Englewood Cliffs, N.J.: Prentice-Hall, 1980.

A survey of organization structure, environment, and behavior and the theories relating their interactions. Based on behavioral surveys, it presents actual findings, their interpretation, and their relationship to the theories.

Mintzberg, Henry. *The Structuring of Organizations.* Englewood Cliffs, N.J.: Prentice-Hall, 1979.

An original work focusing on the diverse aspects of how organizations work in reality. From there, it extracts principles that can help in the structuring of successful organizations.

Ouchi, William. *Theory Z: How American Business Can Meet the Japanese Challenge*. Reading, Mass.: Addison-Wesley, 1981.

Starting with an analysis of the factors behind Japan's industrial success, the author concludes that it is people management, rather than technology, that accounts for it. Then he goes on to propose a theory of people management, using some of the principles that have succeeded in Japan—and in some U.S. companies—adapting them, and extending them to fit the U.S. situation.

Pascale, Richard T., and Athos, Anthony G. *The Art of Japanese Management*. New York: Simon and Schuster, 1981.

Focusing on non-culturally related techniques used by Japanese managers, the authors develop a series of conclusions outlining how American managers can profit from the Japanese experience.

Van de Ven, Andrew H., and Ferry, Diane L. *Measuring and Assessing Organizations*. New York: Wiley, 1980.

Based on the results of a longitudinal research program in progress since 1972, this book proposes an approach to measure and assess organizational effectiveness.

CONCLUSIONS

Kendrick, John W. "Productivity Trends and the Recent Slowdown: Historical Perspective, Causal Factors, and Policy Options." In *Contemporary Economic Problems*. Washington, D.C.: American Enterprise Institute, 1979.

A well-documented paper covering all aspects described in the title.

Leibenstein, Harvey. *Beyond Economic Man*. Cambridge, Mass.: Harvard University Press, 1980.

An original book, introducing explicitly practical nonrational factors into microeconomic analysis. His account of how X-efficiency, manifested as motivation or effort, influences the economic process is extremely useful to understand and describe many aspects of the theory of the firm.

Annotated Videography

The emerging importance of videotapes as means of conveying information has led me to compile this "videography," describing taped materials related to topics covered in this book.

DELTAK, Inc. *Data Base Systems Design*. Oak Brook, Ill.: DELTAK, Inc.

A four-lesson course covering how to evaluate, design, and maintain data base systems.

Drake, Alvin W., and Keeney, Ralph L. *Decision Analysis*. Cambridge, Mass.: Massachusetts Institute of Technology.

A 20-lesson course starting from the basics, proceeding through quantification of uncertainties, dealing with multiple objectives, and including several case studies.

Drucker, Peter F. *Managing Discontinuity*. Rockville, Md.: BNA Communications, Inc.

A series of nine tapes based on Drucker's book. Includes "Tomorrow's Customers," "The Future of Technology," "Coping with Technological Change," "Who's Gonna Collect the Garbage?," "Social Needs as Business Opportunities," "Pollution Control—The Hard Decisions," "The Multinational Corporation," "The Innovative Organization," and "The Manager as Entrepreneur."

Drucker, Peter F. *The Effective Executive*. Rockville, Md.: BNA Communications, Inc.

A series of five tapes covering highlights of Drucker's best-known books. Includes "Managing Time," "What Can I Contribute," "Focus on Tomorrow," "Effective Decisions," and "Staffing for Strength."

Gellerman, Saul W. *Motivation and Productivity*. Rockville, Md.: BNA Communications, Inc.

A series of 10 tapes organized by Gellerman, includes "Strategy for Productive Behavior," "Motivation through Job Enrichment," "The Self-motivated Achiever," "Understanding Motivation," "Theory X and Theory Y, Description," "Theory X and Theory Y, Application," "Human Nature and Organizational Realities," "The Management of Human Assets," and "Motivation in Perspective."

Herzberg, Frederick. *Motivation to Work*. Rockville, Md.: BNA Communications, Inc.

A series of five tapes, including "The Modern Meaning of Efficiency," "KITA, or What Have You Done for Me, Lately," "Job Enrichment in Action," "Building a Climate for Individual Growth," and "The ABC Man: The Manager in Mid-Career."

Martin, James. *Distributed Data Processing: A Management Revolution*. Oak Brook, Ill.: DELTAK, Inc.

A three-lesson course, presenting the basic characteristics of the technology, basic principles for its successful implementation, and potential benefits to be derived from it.

Solomon, Robert D. *Management of Microprocessor Technology*. Cambridge, Mass.: Massachusetts Institute of Technology.

> A course in 10 lessons focusing on five major aspects of microprocessor technology: basics of operation, systems design and development, applications economic impact, new marketing factors and product opportunities, and future hardware and software trends.

Strangio, Christopher E. *Microprocessors: Fundamental Concepts and Applications*. Cambridge, Mass.: Massachusetts Institute of Technology.

> A course in 20 lessons, starting from a basic level, reaching a depth sufficient to design microprocessor software and hardware and evaluate needs and capabilities.

Various authors. *Computer Aided Manufacturing*. Cambridge, Mass.: Massachusetts Institute of Technology.

> A course in 16 lessons, describing the technology, problems, alternative solutions, and state of the art of CAD technology in the United States, Japan, Germany, and Norway.

Index

DATE DUE
